WOMEN WHO

BY LIANE SEBASTIAN

WIN AT WORK

Flowers of wisdom from visionary businesswomen

Published by Frederick Fell Publishers, Inc., Hollywood FL

Thank You

Of the 35 contributors, I knew only six before undertaking this project. A few are often clients: **Cristina Tabora**, **C. Cie Armstead**, **Stephanie Medlock**, and **Marilyn Miglin**. I include my sister, **Jill Sebastian** and several of my idols (admirred since High School): **Alexandra Stoddard, Gloria Steinem** and **Shakti Gawain.** These extraordinary women combine great success professionally, personally, and through their contributions. Special thanks to **Debi Davis** who collaborated greatly!

Gratitude also goes to my grandmother, **Charlotte Sebastian**, who often used the 'Legacy Ladies' phrases, adding a few of her own! This work is dedicated to all the women who made opportunities possible and paved the path for us to win at work!

Thank you to these amazing women who found the fortitude, courage, and conviction to make a difference. Hopefully they will make a difference for you.
— Liane Sebastian, www.prosperiapublishing.com

© copyright 2009
by Liane Sebastian
Published by
Frederick Fell Publishers, Inc.
1403 Shoreline Way
Hollywood, Florida 33019
www.fellpub.com

All Rights Reserved
Library of Congress Catalog
ISBN # 978-088391-184-6
1. Business
2. Businesswomen
3. Womens' Studies
4. Gift

Businesswomen need shortcuts. We rarely have time to learn all that we must to be effective in our work or our lives. Unfortunately, the flood of resources ready to help us can also drown us in too much information. Standing in a bookstore or library, we encounter a multitude of titles with page after page of examples and stories that bury the essential lessons sprinkled throughout. ■

Women who Win at Work is a new kind of resource. It introduces you to hundreds of the best thinkers—most of them authors—with idea-seeds ready to germinate. Each quotation offers practical insight that you can apply to your business immediately. If an idea resonates with you, then the topic will deserve your further exploration. ■

Consider these contributors as friends, teachers, or mentors. Each shares a commitment to cultivate her garden and allow her businesses, projects, and careers to become more fertile. May these leaders help to nurture your own growing enterprise and landscape—so that you, too, can win at work!

WOMEN WHO WIN AT WORK

LEGACY LADIES

Every society has its wise women. We sit at our grandmother's feet, listen to their experience and their council. From the famous achievers, and those that should be famous, these words are treasured like heirloom roses. This collection was begun as favorite sayings drawn on little scraps of colored paper, hung all over a college dorm room wall 30 years ago. Later, spilling out of boxes and envelopes, these idea-seeds have been compiled and edited here to present some of the most classic. The collection is unlimited and you are invited to submit your favorites online.

✳ **The fountain of youth is your mind, your talents, the creativity you bring to your life, and the lives of people you love. When you tap these sources, you defeat age.**
— SOPHIA LOREN

✳ **In life, all good things come hard, but wisdom is the hardest to come by.**
— LUCILLE BALL

✳ **Knowledge helps you make a living; wisdom helps you make a life.**
— SANDRA CAREY

✳ **I feel there is something unexplored about women that only a woman can explore.**
— GEORGIA O'KEEFFE

✳ **It is true we cannot be free from sin, but at least let our sins not always be the same.**
— TERESA OF AVILA

✳ **Every time we liberate a woman, we liberate a man.**
— MARGARET MEAD

✳ **How wonderful it is that nobody need wait a single moment before starting to improve the world.**
— ANNE FRANK

VISIONARY VOICES

These leaders are winners because they balance successful businesses with equally successful and healthy families, communities, and private lives. From all areas of the country and a range of sectors, they define the components that control their fates. They mold business to their personalities and values, thus add to the evolving business climate. They share their wisdom with the hope that they can help you advance more quickly toward your goals. They believe that by helping women in business, they help *all* business.

✳ **Ladies, there is no neutral position for us to assume.**
—GERTRUDE STEIN

✳ **If women understood and exercised their power they could remake the world.**
—EMILY TAFT DOUGLAS

✳ **To learn something new every day is a lofty but achievable goal, because when the student is ready the teacher is always available. While life's lessons may arrive in surprising packages, the gifts of knowledge are always worth opening.**
—ANGELA BEASLEY

JUDITH ANDERSON
business and leadership
consultant, author, NJ
pages 55–57

C. CIE ARMSTEAD
administrative and
leadership executive, IL
pages 107–109

MARTHA BARLETTA
author, advertising and
marketing executive, IL
pages 159–161

COLETTE BARON-REID
intuitive counselor and
singer-song writer, FL
pages 82–83

YVONNE F. BROWN
performance manager,
executive coach, author,
and speaker, IL
pages 36–38

VALERIE BECK
entrepreneur and
association president, IL
pages 24–26

DEBI DAVIS
weight manager,
consultant, author, FL
pages 93–95

MARTHA BOSTON
business consultant,
international trainer,
and coach, TX
pages 112–114

SUSAN DAVIS
consultant for socially
responsible businesses,
association founder, WI
pages 183–185

GERI BRIN
marketing and communica-
tions entrepreneur, NY
pages 84–86

SUZANNE FALTER-BARNS
author, speaker, trainer,
and seminar leader, NY
pages 147–149

DONNA FISHER
author, speaker,
corporate trainer, TX
pages 96–98

ADRIAN GUGLIELMO
entrepreneur and marketer
to special needs communi-
ties, NY
pages 70–72

JULIE GARELLA
investment banker,
entrepreneur, author, NC
pages 121–123

AMY HILLIARD
entrepreneur and
marketing consultant, IL
pages 21–23

MELISSA GIOVAGNOLI
author, knowledge manager,
marketing specialist, IL
pages 162–164

JACKIE HUBA
entrepreneur and author,
TX
pages 198–200

LESLIE GROSSMAN
serial entrepreneur,
marketing consultant,
women's organization
co-founder, NY
pages 186–188

RIEVA LESONSKY
entrepreneur, publisher
and editor, author, CA
pages 45–47

LINDA LISTROM
attorney, partner,
and association leader, IL
pages 138–140

NELL MERLINO
entrepreneur and
community leader, NY
pages 174–176

ANDREA MARCH
trade show strategist and
organization executive,
NY pages 33–35

MARILYN MIGLIN
entrepreneur, author,
and community leader, IL
pages 48–50

GAIL MCMEEKIN
psychotherapist
and author, MA
pages 67–69

SUZANNE PEASE
graphic designer and
association leader, NJ
pages 150–152

STEPHANIE MEDLOCK
educational program
designer and director, IL
pages 79–81

HEDY RATNER
business development
entrepreneur and
community leader, IL
pages 201–203

LEXI REESE
business development and
marketing consultant, NY
pages 171–173

ALEXANDRA STODDARD
interior designer, philosopher of contemporary
living, and author, CN
pages 209–211

LUCY ROSEN
business development and
marketing consultant,
association leader, NY
pages 135–137

CRISTINA TABORA
marketing consultant
and entrepreneur, NY
pages 212–214

JILL SEBASTIAN
educator, artist, and
public art specialist, WI
pages 58–60

ROXANNA TRINKA
surveyor, engineer,
and politician, FL
pages 195–197

ELLEN SHERMAN
marriage and family
therapist, FL
pages 110–111

MELISSA WAHL
organizational director
and consultant, NY
pages 124–126

Women's Strengths

by Liane Sebastian

Why a book for businesswomen? How is our perspective fundamentally different from men's? We all know men who are expressive and compassionate. We all know women who are tough and aggressive. So the differences between men's and women's perspectives are not black and white.

Generally, people should be judged by ability. And most women have unique, untapped abilities. WOMEN WHO WIN AT WORK is a testimony to what women can share and learn from one another. It examines techniques that help us uniquely succeed.

As we grow older, we see patterns in how we limit ourselves. We see how many people are defined by roles. And we learn methods to make decisions that build upon or break our patterns. With perspective gained by working with over 200 clients in 25 years, by employing and not employing staff, and by building a strong personal resumé, I have learned that the gender differences in viewpoints become more pronounced in business. After corresponding or speaking to the contributors in this book, these are the ways they say the majority of women are different from men:

- **Girl friends give as an intimate support structure.** Friendships extend of our lives and help us balance the demands of family and business. We gain strength through *confiding* in others. Men gain strength *doing* things with others.

- **Insatiable inquisitiveness.** We seek personal and professional advice. This book is like having a large group of friends who share knowledge that hopefully is applicable to you. Women's curiosity takes in more variables to process and assimilate into experiences.

- **Master juggling.** Flexibility is a skill learned from negotiating multiple activities and priorities. Few women escape the need to utilize our innate multi-leveled brain structures.

- **Expansive definition of balance.** It is too easy to *lose* balance; most women become acutely aware to both cultivate it and to protect it. Pulled in many directions, virtually all female professionals often feel overwhelmed and exhausted. We develop techniques that help us maintain health, creativity, flexibility, and openness to change.

- **Need of confidence.** Lack of self-esteem victimizes a surprising number of women. Confidence is not something that just happens; it needs to be nurtured. Only then can women become powerful instruments of progress and direct our own destinies.

- **Develop questions.** We need to fully explore options and appreciate the consequences of the choices that influence and affect our lives. It is very serious that so few women understand their financial options. This weakness needs to be addressed before permitting significant progress. Leaders know that our independence is essential—when women excel, everyone excels. A society can be judge by the health and contribution of its women. To build the courage necessary to confront our limitations, we must be honest, adventurous, and stubborn while we preserve our more egalitarian natures.

AUTHORS' ADVICE

There are approximately 200 books on advice specifically by and for businesswomen captured in this collection. Poignant and thought-provoking quotations are presented as idea-seeds. Each of these books may be terrific to read but few workingwomen have time to find the *most* appropriate for them! This collection allows tiny glimpses into larger works; each offers concrete suggestions that we can use today. If one particularly resonates, then read the whole book! With new titles released each year, this body of knowledge can never be complete—but *can* be adapted to the needs of each reader. Additionally they inspire discussion and further exploration. See further reading selections online.

> Leadership is about more than just delivering results—it is about making a difference in the lives of others. The most admired leaders are usually outstanding people-developers who others want to follow.
>
> — Jean Otte, *Changing the Corporate Landscape*

Wisdom is the highest level of emotional, spiritual, and mental evolution, at which you value intuition as much as information, willingness as much as ability, and inspiration as much as knowledge. It is where you synergize your deepest understanding with your everyday actions.

— Chérie Carter-Scott, Ph.D.,
If Life is a Game, These are the Rules

What our politics needs more than anything are the feminine values of nurturing and wisdom. These may have been considered luxuries when men were walking around in saber-toothed tiger pelts carrying clubs, but they have now become essential for our survival.

— Arianna Huffington, *Fanatics & Fools*

Men are promoted based on potential. Women are promoted based on performance. While men are about winning, women are about collaborating in win-win relationships. Women have natural talents like patience, intuition, multi-tasking, networking, and nurturing—powerful leadership qualities for making any business grow. Trust these inbred qualities and use them! Don't try to hide or disguise them!

— Robin Fisher Roffer, *Make a Name for Yourself*

The nature of risk, the ability to build a dream, the reality of creating more with your life requires both debt and invest- ment, and on any given day, the same situation can swing back and forth between the two. The line between debt and investment is frightening, exciting, excruciating, and exhilarating. Experiencing this line is *absolutely* necessary to create wealth.

— Nicole Williams, *Earn What You're Worth*

BALANCE

The wise advise us to equally nurture financial, social, and healthful responsibilities, for if any one area dominates, we lose balance. We can learn and sharpen certain skills that will help to keep balance as our priority. We each need to select our own blend of variables. Clear priorities make the task easier to direct our decisions. Our choices create and define our ecosystem.

LEGACY LADIES

✳ **Happiness is good health and a bad memory.**
— INGRID BERGMAN

✳ **Blessings and Balance, Balance and Blessings, For from Balance comes all Blessings.**
— GRANDMOTHER KEEWAYDINOQUAY, OJIBWAY

✳ **There is a balance between not asking enough of oneself and asking or expecting too much.**
— MAY SARTON

✳ **What is most beautiful in virile men is something feminine; what is most beautiful in feminine women is something masculine.**
— SUSAN SONTAG

This mini-collection represents our roots— wisdom many may have grown up with. These idea-seeds encourage genetic progression: if we share what we know, then we can prepare for storms. Gardens need to be resilient. (See this collection grow online.)

Develop a Balanced Life

by Amy Hilliard

Every businesswoman shares the challenge of balancing often conflicting demands. Rather than allow stress to be the boss, take control of your time:

- **Balance your efforts.** Have more than one focus, but know which has the lead. Then structure the others to be flexible. Learn to dial back and forth as needed.

- **Choose priorities by gut level.** Does the decision feel right, natural, evolving? If change is too much of a stretch or strain, step back, and do not aggressively pursue that direction.

- **Pace the growth of your career or company so you can have a life.** A company that grows slowly allows you to work in time to spend with family and friends.

- **Decide what kind of executive you want to be.** Harvard Business School teaches 'grow, grow, and grow.' It is hard to step away! But look carefully at those who chose that way: it is not like it reads in the books or magazines! Do you want to hug a balance sheet at night?

- **Commitments are most important.** To attend to personal time, exercise, children—prioritizing doesn't mean anything unless you make a commitment. You may look at an item on your list everyday, but it doesn't do any good without taking action.

- **Be honest to find out what works for you.** Spend time by yourself. A woman who is too busy doesn't hear her own voice.

- **Get help. Read. Listen to others.** Emulate women who balance successfully. Ask how they do it.

- **Soft women *can* succeed.** You can remain feminine yet focused. If you do not relinquish your femininity, you are powerful by default. A balanced approach does not intimidate partners. Softer is vulnerable, so friends feel needed. Empathy for employees shows that you know they have lives too. Put a hand on their shoulders when in need, but *do* make them accountable for goals! They won't be loyal to you if you can't be flexible or if you don't stress what is important.

- **Own up to your frailties and admit that you aren't perfect.** Build give-and-take relationships, or others will be resentful. Resentment is a cancer to relationships and avoidable through awareness.

Author of ***Tap Into Your Juices***

Focus your mind on your body. Aches and pains talk to you and say when you are out of balance. Develop a normal foundation of feeling good so you can hear your physical voice talk.

AMY HILLIARD

Ms. Hilliard is the founder, president and CEO of The ComfortCake Company LLC, makers of "pound cake so good it feels like a hug." After successfully launching products for major corporations, Ms. Hilliard decided to try it for herself and her family. In January 2001, she and her team started from "scratch" and stepped into the legacy of her grandfather, an executive chef, to launch the ComfortCake brand. Additionally, Ms. Hilliard is the president of The Hilliard Group, LLC, a strategic marketing consulting and product development firm. Their client list has included IBM, American Express, HBO, Hallmark, Texaco, Chase Manhattan Bank, PepsiCo, Ford, Northwest Airlines, The Gap, Kraft Foods, and *Fortune* magazine, among others. She works in Chicago, IL. Visit www.comfortcake.com.

Spend time by yourself. A woman who is too busy doesn't hear her own voice. Teach your family to understand and encourage their time alone as well.

VALERIE BECK

Ms. Beck is a multiple entrepreneur. She started Chicago Chocolate Tours in 2005 because she loves Chicago, loves chocolate, and loves people. Her organization takes locals, visitors, and groups to chocolate shop favorites as well as tucked-away boutiques. They also provide seated chocolate tastings, gift baskets, Chocolate of the Month Club memberships, and Cocoa Cruises in the Mediterranean. ▪ Ms. Beck is also an Independent Sales Director with Mary Kay. ▪ Prior to becoming an entrepreneur, Ms. Beck practiced as a lawyer in Europe and Chicago firms including Winston & Strawn. Today, she speaks about alternative careers for lawyers at events sponsored by the Chicago Bar Association, *The Law Bulletin*, Northwestern Law School, and her alma mater, Harvard Law School. She also speaks on topics such as how to follow your heart and live authentically. ▪

Ms. Beck contributes to organizations for disadvantaged and at-risk girls both domestically and in impoverished countries. She is active in civic and business organizations including the Chicago Area Chapter of the National Association of Women Business Owners where she serves as the 2009 President. She lives and works in Chicago, IL. Visit:
www.chicagochocolatetours.com
www.romancearoundthecorner.com
www.marykay.com/vbeck

Follow a Golden Thread

by Valerie Beck

A unifying philosophy integrates my three businesses: the golden thread of uplifting experience. After starting out in law, we women attorneys didn't know we were playing a different game than the men. We worked more hours while the men were out building *relationships*. Then we wondered why they got ahead over those of us who did more work! Mary Kay gave me a system that can apply to life as well as to business. The different hats I wear as an entrepreneur are all on the *same* head! To balance activities:

- **Start with your mission.** This is so instilled in my chocolate tour-guides, that if you woke them in the middle of the night and asked about the mission, they would groggily recite: 'uplift through chocolate.' Knowing it so well encourages the team to come up with appropriate ideas and feel they have a stake in our direction.

- **Organize.** Each evening, I list the six most important things to do the next day. These are things that I *get* to do versus *have* to do— I am grateful to run my own business! If any more than six activities I feel overwhelmed. If distracted, the plan can keep me focused.

- **Use feelings as a barometer.** You know that you are doing the right things if your energy is high and time goes by quickly.

- **Get customers involved.** After each tour, attendees receive e-mails to thank them with links where they can obtain their photographs that were taken on the tour.

- **Contribute.** If you have the *why* then the *how* is not so scary. Let your business make visible that which without you would be invisible. You can fall down and get up again; the why keeps you going.

- **Create momentum.** If you are not moving forward, you're moving backwards.

- **Control pace.** The chocolate tour business is growing and I want to expand to other cities. But now would be too much too soon. It is important to build *one* baby before building others!

- **Plan.** I use a week-at-a-glance planning sheet to plot out my activities. Like Mary Kay said: if *you* don't plan your time, someone else will! I use different colors to make plans visual and rough in chunks of time.

- **Determine control.** The hardest part of business is not *outside* of me—though it may be tempting to think so. The hardest part is to take responsibility for what I *can* control.

- **Get sleep!** If you sacrifice your health, what balance can you have? With sleep, you can feel more in control.

To find a need and fill it is the most exciting part of business. Mary Kay said that people won't come to you for your name and your fame. They will come to you because you help them with a need they must solve. The golden thread equals giving to create the richest life.

Author of ***Romance Around the Corner: Eight Steps Towards Attracting tghe Man of Your Dreams***

You find balance in knowing what *matters* to you. Then you live your life accordingly and won't need to seek 'work/life balance.'

— Andrea Kay,
Work's a Bitch and Then You Make it Work

The time I take away from my work makes my time at work all the more productive.

— Beverly Kaye and Sharon Joran-Evans,
Love It, Don't Leave It

"

Successful people create a balance that energizes, refreshes, and renews them every day. Their balancing act isn't perfect, and it requires constant attention—but they are vigilant about maintaining it because they appreciate the continuity between home and rest, work and productivity. If you are refreshed and balanced, you will have more energy and be more productive.

— Julie Morgenstern, *Making Work* Work

"

The woman who feels whole has a sense of self based on multiple identities—manager, negotiator, spouse, confidante, mother, implementer, and nurturer. Feelings of wholeness are often achieved after much soul-searching and restructuring to identify and integrate priorities. It is a process that never really ends, as wholeness requires active maintenance.

— Marian N. Ruderman and Patricia J. Ohlott,
Standing at the Crossroads

The biggest mistake I ever made in any job was letting the job take over my life.… When I began channeling less energy into the job and more into my private life, what surprised me is that my work didn't suffer. When it got rough at work, I had something else going on to distract me.

— Kelly Love Johnson, *Skirt Rules > For the Workplace*

"

We must give whatever it is
we want to receive. If we want
more cooperation and respect,
we must be cooperative and
respective. If success (however
we define it) is our goal, then
we should help others to succeed. If we want more joy, we
must be more joyful. When
we give from our hearts, when
we give in a spirit of love and
compassion, we receive even
more than we give.

— Mary Mitchell, *Class Acts*

"

CONFIDENCE

Few are born with confidence; most of us must earn it. Cultivating experience can bolster an independent self and lessen the need for nurturing or reinforcement from others. Only a sound internal architecture can withstand the currents and storms of change. Confidence gives us assurance both to handle any circumstance, and to continually harvest our resources.

LEGACY LADIES

✳ **If you risk nothing, then you risk everything.**
— GEENA DAVIS

✳ **How many cares one loses when one decides not to be some*thing*, but to be some*one*.**
— COCO CHANEL

✳ **It's more important what's *in* a woman's face than what's *on* it.**
— CLAUDETTE COLBERT

✳ **Friendship with oneself is all-important, because without it one cannot be friends with anyone else.**
— ELEANOR ROOSEVELT

This mini-collection represents our roots—wisdom many may have grown up with. These idea-seeds encourage genetic progression: if we share what we know, then we can prepare for storms. Gardens need to be resilient. (See this collection grow online.)

Entrepreneurial Essentials

by Andrea March

Confidence is the most important ingredient to success. Without it, you don't think you'll succeed—and so, most likely, you won't. Confidence plus passion are also the two most important ingredients to being an entrepreneur. To cultivate:

- **Use introspection.** Become both in touch with yourself and with a need that you believe in. Develop a staunch inner belief and strength for determining your direction.

- **Become consumed.** When excitement and passion grow, each gains momentum. To achieve something meaningful, eat and sleep your project! Follow your special talent and take the leap.

- **Be responsive.** Passion comes from the belief that you'll get a buy-in from supporters and that the market will accept your idea. Do your homework and be current with industry developments. Knowledge propels conviction and is a tool for confidence.

- **Be open to learn.** Educational institutions do not meet the needs of business people. Partners, mentors, and other learning venue such as conferences and seminars, are better alternatives.

- **Look beyond the start.** Although confidence and passion are enough to *start* a project or a business, you need other talents and skills to implement them. Confidence enables you to approach others with your vision. You can't imagine how your market could *not* want or even live without your product! However, like how terrible movies get produced, confidence and passion alone are not enough to make a viable enterprise.

- **Market sensibly.** Know your customer, know your industry, know that your product is crucial to the well-being of your constituents, and you can develop the perseverance needed for business challenge. Quality and concern for the market have to take dominance.

- **Everyone must sell.** Confidence and passion come naturally to some. A successful sales person who *believes* in her products can express this passion contagiously to others.

- **Present yourself.** When you meet someone new, likability is key—personality, appearance, etc. Develop your own Interview Checklist. This list doesn't just work for interviews, but it works for life. Put your best foot forward everyday. Dress the part. Be on time, etc. Every day is another interview!

The most rewarding business will address your passions and grievances—and resonate with others. It must blend your talents, skills, and conviction.

ANDREA MARCH

Ms. March is a serial entrepreneur who has successfully reinvented herself several times as a woman business owner and leader. Co-founding the Women's Leadership Exchange (WLE), she says, is the fulfillment of her destiny, the culmination of all her previous experience.

After receiving a degree from New York University, Ms. March sold real estate and then partnered with her husband in a highly successful jewelry import and distribution company. After 20 years of building the multi-million dollar business, she realized that she did not have a clue about understanding the language of investment! With serendipitous circumstances, Ms. March started Investment Expo, an innovative trade show/seminar program (www.investmentexpo.com) that grew into one of the leading providers of financial information in the U.S.

In 2002, Leslie Grossman (see page 186) attended one of Ms. March's two-day events. The two share a powerful commitment to women entrepreneurs like themselves. Thus, they created WLE to provide "the tools, interactive mentoring, access to money or sponsors, and most of all, the networking that could help take our already significant businesses to an even higher level. It is growing because it meets a real need and is doing well while doing good." She lives and works in New York. Visit www.womensleadershipexchange.com.

YVONNE F. BROWN

Ms. Brown is Chief Empowerment Officer of JAD Communications International, a motivational training and human potential firm. She is also President of Ball of Gold Corporation, a knowledge management, consultancy and training company. During her over 25 years in business, she managed major U.S. and foreign business initiatives with diverse teams. She assists companies with cultural difference education programs and leadership strategies. Ms. Brown holds a Bachelors of Arts degree in Business Management from DePaul University and an Associate of Applied Science from the College of DuPage. She is an author, sought after keynote speaker, and was an adjunct professor at the University of Illinois at Chicago for the MBA Professional Development Program office. ■ As a graduate of the Leadership Illinois Class she was recently elected to the Steering Committee for the Chicago Minority Business Development Council. ■ Ms. Brown helps people to stop self-limiting beliefs, eliminate self-sabotage, and reach their highest potential. She lives and works in Chicago, IL. Visit www.jadcommunications.com.

Exude Confidence

by Yvonne F. Brown

Confidence. The word conjures up images of self-assurance and belief in ones' self. Self-confidence is inward security, integrity to your own value system. It is not congruent with doubt or fear. 'Confidence thrives only on honesty, on honor, on the sacredness of obligations, on faithful protection, and on unselfish performance. Without these, it cannot live.' (Franklin D. Roosevelt.) It is an essential beginning to any pursuit. To develop, remember:

- **Confidence can be acquired.** It is not an inherent part of personality, but can be learned, honed, and integrated into daily behavior.

- **Don't let losing become a habit.** Circumstances don't matter. You are in control of how you react to and deal with every situation.

- **Confidence is built or lost by choice.** It can be destroyed or enhanced by a parent, teacher, sibling, or colleague— through an offhand remark taken to heart and integrated into the psyche of the receiver.

- **Challenge lack of confidence.** If you have low self-esteem, luckily you can find the direction to build it up if motivated.

- **Pursue research and education.** Know your material and you only have to overcome the reluctance of getting up in front of an audience. Step up and *act* as if you are a great speaker! The audience can't tell that you have butterflies in your stomach!

- **Incubate the situation.** Step back and reflect, but don't make a decision yet. Consider ways to restructure the situation. Hold it up to the light and look for opportunities.

- **Take action.** Begin by acting as if you are self-confident with something small. Pretend and just *do* whatever it is you are nervous about doing. After preparation, assume the attitude that you would like to have.

- **Integrate.** Incorporate the new behavior in your daily actions. As time passes, your confidence will grow. So, believe in yourself! Have faith in your abilities! Without a humble (but reasonable) confidence in your own powers, you cannot be successful or happy.

Author of ***Self Creation: 10 Powerful Principles for Changing Your Life; Frederick Douglass: Master Self Creator***

When making a presentation, become immersed enough in your passion for your subject that you overcome the jitters.

Self-esteem makes life a bed of roses instead of a brier patch. To assume that somebody else can make you happy is to give away power. Women are taught to please others, but security is not built solely upon love and approval. 'Security' is an illusion. The closest we can come to it is the knowledge that we can handle our lives without outside help.

— Juliet Nierenberg,
Women and the Art of Negotiating

By reeducating the mind, you can accept fear as simply a fact of life rather than a barrier to success. To diminish your fear is to develop more trust in your ability to handle whatever comes your way! The only way to get rid of the fear of doing something is to go out and do it. Pushing through fear is less frightening than living with the underlying fear that comes from a feeling of helplessness.

— Susan Jeffers, Ph.D.,
Feel the Fear and Do It Anyway

Once we receive criticism, we must also guard against it destroying us. We should not allow our internal dialogue to become negative; rather, we should use the information for what it's worth and then proceed with our lives. Use praise to help further your position in the hierarchy. Extend praise for the benefit of your career.

— Pat Heim, Ph.D., *Hardball for Women*

If you want to get noticed by the right people, strut your stuff. Show up at places where your presence will remind the people who matter that you're definitely in the mix. Wear something fantastic and introduce (or reintroduce) yourself to anyone in a position to change your destiny.

— Kate White, *Nine Secrets of Women Who Get Everything They Want*

"

Accept yourself as you are.
We all make mistakes and
lots of them. The sooner you
figure out that your mistakes
don't define you any more
than your successes, the
sooner you'll be able to
accept them as the crucial
part of the learning process
that they are.

— Poppy King, *Lessons of a Lipstick Queen*

VITALITY

Energy and time embody two of our most valuable resources. Having enough energy to make the best use of time propagates the foundation of vitality. Healthy habits, an organized environment, and prosperity are like compost for that foundation. How we feel determines the level at which we operate. Providing our landscape with the nutrients needed to grow, vitality is the measure of health—physically, emotionally, financially, and corporately.

LEGACY LADIES

✳ **It is the mind that makes the body.**
— SOJOURNER TRUTH

✳ **As long as my body is in shape,
my mind is working at its full capacity.**
— VICTORIA PRINCIPAL

✳ **People who drink to drown their sorrow
should be told that sorrow knows how to swim.**
— ANN LANDERS

✳ **Careful grooming may take twenty years
off a woman's age, but you can't fool
a long flight of stairs.**
— MARLENE DIETRICH

This mini-collection represents our roots—wisdom many may have grown up with. These idea-seeds encourage genetic progression: if we share what we know, then we can prepare for storms. Gardens need to be resilient. (See this collection grow online.)

The Way to 'Have It All'

by Rieva Lesonsky

You *can* do everything you want to do, but you can't do it all at the same time! If you can shift the percentages of what is important, you will achieve all of your goals. Question how things have always been done. Break societal habits to develop techniques that work best for you:

- **Develop a good method for setting priorities.** Don't plan only for the long-term. Most women have to evaluate their activities daily. Use whatever planning frequency is comfortable (daily, weekly, monthly) but *stick* to it! You will gain momentum.

- **Keep activities flexible to situation.** If you want to go to your child's game that week, maybe you have to rearrange tasks and work a little extra. Practice shifting gears in both life *and* business. Once you learn this flexibility, you feel better about all you have to do.

- **Create and use a business plan.** Some entrepreneurs succeed without a plan by taking advantage of a lucky situation: they happen to be in the right place at the right time. If you are lucky *and* smart *and* you manage a successful fad well, you *might* be able to build beyond early good fortune. Your lucky methods might work okay at first, but not after about three years when referrals and resources have been stretched. *Then* a plan is critical. It encapsulates your vision, is a foundation so you know what to do, and helps you reach where you want to go. There are *very few* overnight successes!

- **Collaborate with clients.** Entrepreneurs can have trouble accepting that the client is boss. They often start their own businesses to be their *own* bosses! But they have to do things the client's way and not necessarily their own way. Successful entrepreneurs *collaborate* with clients to find solutions that work to mutual benefit. When the client is set up as the boss and the entrepreneur as the server, you end up with a business transaction. But business actually builds on *relationships* through deals that work for both. This is not an either/or proposition. With creativity and focus, there can *always* be a win/win arrangement to satisfy both parties. This *does* take work! Even Bill Gates failed two times with earlier Windows operating systems! Then he went to the user, took egos off the table, and asked why they hated the early versions. He collaborated with his customers, and then tried again.

Awareness *plus* luck *plus* a plan *plus* the ability to follow your gut are the ingredients for the successful entrepreneur who can find a good balance between these variables. To 'have it all' really means adjusting your success to take advantage of your situation.

Co-authored ***Start Your Own Business***, ***Young Millionaires***, and ***303 Marketing Tips***; and authored ***Get Smart***.

You can do everything you want to do, but you can't do it all at the same time! If you can shift the percentages of what is important, you will achieve all of your goals. Choose your pace. How you grow your business is within your control. Concentrate on activities that will help your business the most.

RIEVA LESONSKY

In the upper echelon of business magazines, males rule. The exception is *Entrepreneur* where Ms. Lesonsky served as the senior vice president and editorial director, one of the first and only women ever to hold a top editorial spot at a general business magazine. Since 1987, she was at the helm of Entrepreneur Media. Each month, millions turned to Ms. Lesonsky and her staff for advice, guidance, and inspiration. ■ Ms. Lesonsky has served on the Small Business Administration's National Advisory Council, was honored as a Small Business Media Advocate, and a Woman in Business Advocate. A nationally recognized speaker and expert on small business and entrepreneurship, Ms. Lesonsky appears on numerous national radio and TV programs, including *Good Morning America, Oprah*, and the *Today Show.* ■ She holds a bachelor's degree in journalism from the University of Missouri, Columbia, and held research positions for a major Los Angeles publisher, as well as at Doubleday & Co. in New York City. ■ Originally wanting a career in journalism to help change the world, Ms. Lesonsky fulfilled that dream at *Entrepreneur*. Now she fulfills her dream to have her own business to help other women entrepreneurs. She lives and works in Los Angeles. Visit www.askrieva.com.

MARILYN MIGLIN

Ms. Miglin is among the nation's top-500 women business owners. Her signature fragrance, Pheromone, is among the top-10 fragrances sold in luxury department stores nationwide and each month, more than 65 million television viewers invite her into their homes to purchase her products. Her list of achievements and honors, including the Raoul Wallenberg International Humanitarian Award, are many, but she is particularly beloved for what she gives back to the community. A founding member of the University of Illinois' advisory board for the Craniofacial Center, she is widely recognized for her work with the facially disfigured and burn survivors. In addition, she is well-known for her efforts in establishing the Women of Destiny mentoring program for aspiring young professional women. Ms. Miglin is a formidable force on the side of charity and civic leadership—so much so, that Chicago's most fashionable shopping boulevard is now officially named the "Marilyn Miglin Way." She lives in Chicago, IL. Visit www.marilynmiglin.com.

There are enough stresses in all working-women's lifestyles. If you deal with those that are extraneous, controlling the important ones becomes much easier!

Sustain an Organized Lifestyle

by Marilyn Miglin

No professional woman has enough time. Pulled in many different directions, she needs all the help she can get. But there are ways she can help herself every day that she may not be using. Here are tips for how women can reduce stress through personal organization:

- **Take care of maintenance.** Covering up for chipped nails, torn stockings, unpolished shoes, or a messy kitchen all add unnecessary stresses. With efficient solutions to these tasks, you can stay ahead of them, and your stress will lessen. Concentrate on getting your face, body, living space, and clothes all in order. You will feel better about your other tasks.

- **Make order by category.** Tackle one aspect of your environment such as your shoes. Weed them out. Polish and repair them all at once. Every time you dress, your shoes will be in shape, ready to go. Get rid of shoes that you haven't worn in a year. You *won't* wear them so why *intend* to?

- **Clean out closets and drawers.** Recycle. Donate. Closets affect attitude: they make you feel prepared or disheveled. How you use your active storage has to do with how the rest of your life proceeds. Make sure nothing is in there you haven't used for six months. Don't mix active and deep storage. Develop a system and ritual for weeding out.

- **Get help.** Personal shoppers do not cost more and they get to know your needs. They can save you time when you are planning and strategically adding to your wardrobe. They can help you stay current and excited without requiring much time to implement.

- **Control how much you touch.** Learn systems to manage clutter so you focus on each object only once. Keep folders that are organized around decisions you make about each piece of paper. Designate a place for each category of material you receive and stick to it.

- **Organize reading material.** Designate specific time to deal with it such as when traveling (you can throw more away than you arrived with).

- **Find ways to lighten your load.** Travel with old clothes that you can leave behind—many hotels can funnel to appropriate donations.

- **Have a 'next' table** to hold books you intend to read and tapes you intend to listen to. Let this *one* table be what bothers you and find solace in your organization everywhere else.

- **Practice key preparation.** Whenever you need to leave your home or hotel room, prepare your environment for whenever you come back.

- **Organize, organize, organize!** Start with your thoughts. This creates actions which create force with energy and momentum.

Such necessities are the foundation of a pleasant demeanor. By taking care of the details, your thoughts are able to better focus on what matters versus what annoys.

Author of: ***Best Face Forward***

Take ownership of your schedule and priorities to use time the way you choose rather than the way others choose for you.

"

There is no substitute for the self-confidence and security that financial stability provides us. When we earn at our potential, we can follow our ambition where it leads us and achieve amazing goals. When we earn enough, we know deep down that we can do or handle anything that comes our way, [that we] are fundamentally in charge of our own lives.

— Mikelann R. Valterra, *Why Women Earn Le$$*

"

Hiking, swimming, tennis, or any type of regular physical activity is crucial. Twenty minutes of a sustained cardiovascular workout changes brain activity and begins pulling us out of a depression. Regular exercise is important to the mental health of anyone who spends most of her time engaged in creative work.

— C. Diane Ealy, Ph.D.,
A Woman's Book of Creativity

"

The biggest gains in fitness come from doing *something* instead of nothing. Sure, the gains become even greater if you push yourself to do more. But there's a much more dramatic change in endurance and strength when you go from being sedentary to moderately active than from moderately active to very active.

— Miriam E. Nelson, Ph.D.,
The Strong Women's Journal

"

CREATIVITY

Not just the purview of artists, creative insight empowers all professionals to find new business solutions—especially flexible and scalable options that women so badly need. Creativity expands with practice. Capture and hone the skills needed to transform worthy ideas into reality. To develop the seeds of creativity, carefully choose where to plant and when to harvest. Creativity is the essence of growth.

LEGACY LADIES

✳ **Life is very nice, but it lacks form. It's the aim of art to give it some.**
— JEAN ANOUILH

✳ **Nothing you write, if you hope to be any good, will ever come out as you first hoped.**
— LILLIAN HELLMAN

✳ **Writing is like making love. Don't worry about the orgasm, worry about the process.**
— ISABEL ALLENDE

✳ **Everyone has talent. What is rare is the courage to follow that talent to the dark place where it leads.**
— ERICA JONG

This mini-collection represents our roots—wisdom many may have grown up with. These idea-seeds encourage genetic progression: if we share what we know, then we can prepare for storms. Gardens need to be resilient. (See this collection grow online.)

The Garden of Our Experience

by Judith Anderson

For a flower to reach its full potential, it must have space to grow and access to nutrients. Weeds compete and can slow down the growth process through crowding. For people to grow and bloom and reach our full potential, the elimination of weeds is one aspect of cultivation for which we can take responsibility:

- **Make choices.** As a process, we choose what relationships, belief structures, and concerns allow us to grow more easily or make it more difficult for us to reach our full potential.

- **Discriminate.** As we cultivate our life garden, stop investing in relationships that do not serve us, reframe limiting beliefs, and heal the concerns that hold us back from achieving our life purpose. In this process of questioning, our attitude toward weeds is as important as the cultivation process itself.

- **Weeds are not good or bad.** When we demand that the weeds 'go away and not come back,' they become an irritation. We think that the presence of a weed means something is wrong. All of a sudden we are 'pulling weeds' instead of cultivating our gardens. Instead of treasuring the blossoms, we might see only what we don't want— the weeds. We become destroyers, not creators. Energetically, we hurt our gardens as we hurl these thoughts into the earth: we contaminate the soil and our experience—joy and beauty are interrupted.

- **Determine what is and what is not a weed.** Weeds are any plants growing where we don't want them. Each gardener decides what is a weed and what is a flower. This definition can even change daily! When we take responsibility to cultivate, we choose what to grow and nurture. We choose how to invest time and energy. When in accordance with a life purpose, this can be an easy and graceful process. When not in accordance with a life purpose, we can feel lost and overcome by circumstances, being crowded by what we don't want.

- **Evaluate and eliminate.** When cultivating, there may come times when we see that a habit, belief, or relationship is no longer serving us, and we choose to weed it out. We can see this as a creative process, as making room for more of what we *do* want. There is no need to judge the habit, belief, or relationship as 'wrong' or 'bad.' Such an attitude only lowers the quality of life. Instead, we can lovingly and positively cultivate our paths.

- **Acknowledge and nurture.** Cultivation is not only about elimination; it is also about regarding with loving kindness what the creative process brings forward. Spending time to acknowledge and appreciate what is in our garden creates enthusiasm and motivation for the *entire* creative process—both of cultivation *and* idea generation.

Author of ***The Path to Corporate Nirvana:
An Enlightened Approach to Accelerated Productivity***

*Each gardener decides for herself
what is a weed and what is a flower.
This definition may change daily!*

JUDITH ANDERSON

Ms. Anderson is the co-founder of two businesses: Anderson & Rust (business consulting) and LeadershipU.org (a leadership development organization). She has 25 years of business experience in strategic planning, quantitative analysis, and marketing with an emphasis on the enlightened approach to accelerated productivity in the workplace. She brings unique strengths to the task of helping companies achieve meaningful business results while facilitating individual and team development. ■ Ms. Anderson has held positions with several industry advisory groups, including a three-year research project at Michigan State University on global best practices, and was a member of the Executive Committee for the Council of Logistics Management. She holds a Master of Science degree in Economics and a Master of Arts degree in Spiritual Psychology. Prior to founding Anderson & Rust, Ms. Anderson served as director of Marketing for Ryder System. During the mid-1970's, she worked with Mercer Management Consultants. Ms. Anderson also served as director of Corporate Planning for Union Pacific Corporation. She works in Allendale, NJ. Visit www.andersonrust.com.

JILL SEBASTIAN

Professor Sebastian's sculpture and installations are exhibited across the United States in museums and galleries. She has been represented by galleries in New York, Birmingham, Los Angeles; and is currently with Michael Lord Gallery. ■ Her major public works include sculptural portals in the Midwest Express Center, Milwaukee, and many public park installations. Major commissions have included a lakefront apartment building mosaic/bronze sculpture, a mosaic environment for the Biotech Center at the University of Wisconsin, and an integrated streetscape for State Street in Madison. ■ Professor Sebastian speaks at universities and conferences in the U.S. and Europe. She advises a Mel Chin Percent for Art project in the San Jose Library and organizes a three-day Midwest conference "Beyond the Object: Public Art."

Additionally, she serves on the Milwaukee Arts Board, the Riverwalk Development Committee, and the advisory committee of the Wisconsin Arts Board. ■ She studied at the University of Wisconsin, Northern Illinois University, and received her Masters degree from the University of Wisconsin-Milwaukee. Professor Sebastian has taught sculpture at the University of Denver before joining the Milwaukee Institute of Art and Design faculty in 1989. She lives and works in Milwaukee, WI. Visit www.miad.edu.

The Character of Creativity

by Jill Sebastian

Many myths surround creativity. Anyone who wishes to harness innovative power, both individually or through collaborations, would do well to consider the real components of a challenging quest:

- **Creativity is not only problem solving.** It is a process by which you gather what you know and connect them in new ways. Intuition is cultivated by use and built by direct experience. Solutions are creative when the process to arrive at them blends not-so-uncommon ingredients.

- **Individuality informs creativity.** Everyone is unique. Creativity is given fertile soil when you are honest with yourself, identify your gifts, and most importantly, apply them. You can compensate for your shortcomings with discerning research and a willingness to try something new.

- **Inspiration is hard work.** Rather than divine intervention, creativity exercised regularly becomes habit—the foundation of inspired work. You can cultivate this habit by asking 'What if . . .' and acting on the unexpected with perseverance.

- **Limitations are opportunities.** When a sculptor tries to defy gravity she ignores her most formative ally. The principle of embracing an obstacle is as relevant in the creative struggle as it is in the martial arts. The problem inevitably leads to the solution.

- **Focus on the process not the solution.** Think of time as a malleable fixed material like clay. This is true whether a creative engagement is for an individual or for a group. Too often committees start by focusing on the efficiency of getting the job done without taking the time to share or learn from one another's' expertise. It is worth the time initially to observe, listen, and reflect. The resolution can so often feel like it almost forms itself if the concept and direction are clear!

- **Learn to identify a good idea.** Suspend judgment in the beginning to brainstorm freely with yourself and with others. Don't rule out unconventional ideas just because they're new. Once you think you have something, strip it to its essence, its core concept, and then rebuild it. Fluff will dissipate but a good idea can withstand tests and grow into a great one.

- **Courage can't be avoided but can be effectively acquired within the process.** Fear to begin, fear to look foolish, fear to be criticized, fear to fail—everyone is subject to self-doubt. Sometimes taking the creative first step means pretending outwardly to have a confidence you are not sure you possess inwardly. Uncertainty pales before a well-developed premise—the passion of a good idea. The repeated process of creative conceptualization and implementation of ideas builds vision and direction. With them, the courage and fortitude to continue will develop.

The collective creativity of committees, panels, and collaborations follows the same principles as those of individual exploration. Viewing collective activity as simply a shortcut to combine expertise from limited contributions is doomed to failure. A commitment to quality as an expression of personal and/or community values is essential at the beginning to give purpose, and finally at the end to measure the process and success.

Solutions are creative when the process to arrive at them blends common ingredients.

You can always find a different way to go about getting what you want. Keep an open mind and look for new approaches. It is not about how to slice up the pie (convince) or how to expand the pie (collaborate). It's about baking cakes instead of pies, or buying them instead of baking them yourself.

— Lee E. Miller and Jessica Miller,
A Woman's Guide to Successful Negotiating

Draw out great ideas through:

1. strategic questions—to help people reframe situations.

2. soliciting the clash of ideas for the full range of possibilities.

3. raw facts and unfiltered opinion. Speak last, not first, so people will not unconsciously conform their thinking to yours.

4. a focus on the quality of what emerges, rather than on the time spent.

— Stephanie Winston, *Organized for Success*

Do you want your culture determined by other people? By participating—going to see art, supporting what we think has value, and talking about it—we can define our world. If you want art to say something to you, get out there and strike up a conversation with it.

— Alison Bing, as quoted by Lauren Catuzzi Grandcolas, *You Can Do It!*

Focus on a problem and then generate as many radical solutions as you can. Ideas should deliberately be as broad and odd as possible, and they should be developed as fast as possible. Brainstorming is a lateral-thinking process: it is designed to help you break out of habitual thinking patterns and into new ways of looking at things.

— Caitlin Friedman and Kimberly Yorio,
The Girl's Guide to Starting Your Own Business

Fear is the natural companion of creative action. Do it right, do it wrong, but do it. You will never learn or accomplish or create anything of value if you cannot let yourself make mistakes.... You never feel really bad when you've given something your best show.

— Barbara Sher, *Wishcraft: How to Get What You Really Want*

PASSION

People tend to react emotionally before they react rationally. Any venture that does not capture and direct the passion of its creator will not resonate in the hearts of its audience—only efforts fueled by deep conviction convey passionate meaning. Passion at its best is constructive, for passion gives the power to initiate, to accomplish, and to complete. Passion permeates the very soil that hides beneath the foliage it supports.

LEGACY LADIES

✳ **Life loves the liver of it.**
— MAYA ANGELOU

✳ **Take all away from me, but leave me Ecstasy,**
And I am richer then than all my Fellow Men.
— EMILY DICKINSON

✳ **Woman's discontent increases in**
exact proportion to her development.
— ELIZABETH CADY STANTON

✳ **To love life for some men is to love fighting,**
for fighting, and not love, is seen as
man's deepest passion.
— JOYCE CAROL OATES

This mini-collection represents our roots—wisdom many may have grown up with. These idea-seeds encourage genetic progression: if we share what we know, then we can prepare for storms. Gardens need to be resilient. (See this collection grow online.)

An Inner Way of Knowing

by Gail McMeekin

Intuition is your internal information and feeling source—an inner library of physical and emotional cues that can direct you onto the right avenue. It is the composite of 'gut feelings' and perceptions unique to you. Too often, we are trained to discount or repress this knowledge and to purposely neglect it, devalue it, or refuse to recognize its message. But intuition is a tool for insight and illumination. To develop, sharpen, and use it requires skills in listening to yourself:

- **Keep a creative journal** for answering your exploratory questions. You may be surprised at the wisdom and guidance stored in seemingly random thoughts. Write down everything and anything that comes to mind.

- **Use exploratory inquiry as a fundamental reality-check.** What do you feel excited by? What kinds of books or magazines do you read? What kinds of people do you most like to engage with? What interests or projects are you drawn to in leisure? If you went back to school, what would you most like to learn? Do you long to paint or write or build or organize or sing? What does your internal voice urge you to explore or experience? No idea is wrong or silly.

- **Evaluate the past in relation to the future.** Clear away the past to facilitate the new. What regrets do you have about lost opportunities? What creative dreams have you abandoned and why? List all the things you wanted to do, but didn't. Then think back to what your intuition told you about each option. Think back to when you were clear that a particular choice was not a wise one. What has happened when you hushed up your intuitive warnings and moved forward anyway? Such lessons can fuel your determination to honor your intuitive doubts in the future, to trust, follow, and grow your intuition. Make peace with these cast offs. What can you learn from them? What does your inner voice tell you about these choices now? Grieve what you must and then turn the corner to make room for the next episode.

- **Assess the situation.** You are grateful to your intuition for _____ [fill in with your example]. When has your inner voice steered you right? List the times when it helped you make the best decision or prompted you to try something beneficial. What have you learned about how intuition operates on your behalf?

- **Find new combinations.** Note any patterns that are still possible for an enduring vision that you want to manifest. What options open if you combine an old dream with new skills and experiences? It may not be too late for you to pursue some of the paths not taken.

- **Have faith in your direction.** Learn to trust your intuition as the critical foundation for creativity.

Author of *The 12 Secrets of Highly Creative Women: A Portable Mentor* and *The Power of Positive Choices*

When you grasp meaning as an individual, you can create a travel itinerary for your life's journey— a framework to make choices and direct efforts.

GAIL MCMEEKIN

With more than twenty-five years of experience helping clients discover and achieve their personal, professional, and creative goals, Ms. McMeekin specializes in empowering women to fulfill their creative potential. As a licensed psychotherapist, career coach, human resources consultant, and writer, she has a wealth of knowledge and insight to share.

Ms. McMeekin has a Bachelor of Arts from Connecticut College, an M.S.W. from Boston University, and a certificate in Human Resources from Bentley College. Her work has been featured in *Redbook, Shape, Woman's Day, The Boston Globe, Investor's Business Daily, New Age,* and on America Online as well as radio and television programs. She works in Newton Centre, MA. Visit www.creativesuccess.com.

> *Today's workplace requires you to invoke new answers, innovate, and discover creative solutions.*

ADRIAN GUGLIELMO

Ms. Guglielmo is a veteran of the specialty advertising industry and a member of the Women's Business Enterprise National Council. She was recently honored with an Enterprising Women of the Year Award. In 2001 Ms. Guglielmo was the New York City Woman-Run Business Success Story and won the Inspirational Achievement Award from the Long Island Women's Business Association. ■ The grandchild of a deaf couple, Ms. Guglielmo volunteers among the disabled and disadvantaged. Owning and operating Diversity Partners she became the leading marketer to diverse and special-needs communities for many Fortune 1,000 companies. ■ Ms. Guglielmo works in New York City. Having lost her business in the World Trade Center on 9/11, 2001, she rebuilt through the support of loyal clients and employees. ■ She then teamed up with Kathryn Murphy to create Promotional Services for Artists With Disabilities. Hundreds of artists from all over the country offer promotional and premium items to businesses, large and small. Some projects involve corporations such as Johnson & Johnson, McDonald's, Manhattan Cruise Lines, ADP as well as casinos including Caesar's Palace and Bally's. Visit www.vsf-usa.org.

Promote with Passion

by Adrian Guglielmo

It is always unnerving to approach a prospective client. But it is essential for success—especially entrepreneurial success. There are specific ways to ensure a rewarding client experience:

- **Love what you do** and make it flexible to what you like. If you have no passion, get out of what you are doing very quickly! Let your passion lead you to more fulfilling explorations.

- **Direct passion to your work and your friends; then the success will come.** There is no such thing as a quick buck. Work hard. Money is no motivator; for it is not sustaining. Without passion you will not still be standing at the end of the economic battle. Those who are only motivated by money lack conviction.

- **Be prepared.** First find out about the prospective client. Doing your homework will help you form good questions and demonstrate your sincerity. It saves time by giving you an insight to build upon.

- **Listen carefully.** It is better not to offer anything before you hear what a prospect has to say. Then find an angle on your product or service that will work for *them*.

- **Relate through experiences; connect through values.** Try to find commonalities without pretension.

- **Be positive and open.** Begin a business relationship in an environment that is clean and crystal clear. Don't bring in any skeletons from the past.

- **Eliminate any sexual energy.** If you flirt, men have to flirt. It can ruin a deal and undermine efforts to connect on a deeper, more sustaining level.

- **Treat all situations as an even playing field.** Deal with men and women equally. Approach others as sisters—as you want them to approach you.

- **Be flexible.** If you only have one product, you are in trouble unless your item can reach many people on many levels. Learn to sell your idea sixteen different ways!

- **Speak with passion and conviction.** Passion shows immediately. If you are passionate, mistakes are forgiven and good deeds are elevated.

Take all that is in your heart—from the love of children to the love of your job—and bring that passion into your actions. Do whatever it takes to speak from the heart. Just getting up to speak will take you to the next step. The mousiest people can bring the most passion to their words because it is hard and because it is a risk to do so. Learn that if you don't speak, you automatically lose.

When in touch with your passion, you have energy, vitality, and creativity. Find conscious ways to design more of what you love into your everyday existence. Recognize who you are passionate about *being* rather than just what you are passionate about *doing*. The broader your area of passion the more places you can express it.

— Marcia Wieder, *Doing Less and Having More*

You lose power when you are involved in activities not connected to your passion. Pause to ensure that your priorities are in order. Optimize talents by focusing on your strengths and neutralizing your weaknesses. If you aren't clear about who you are and what you want, no one else will be either.

— Trudy Bourgeois, *Her Corner Office*

WOMEN WHO WIN AT WORK • © 2009 Liane Sebastian

The highest career risk comes with not being comfortable with the merits of your ability and style. Women who take risks trust their own instincts, even under direct challenge. They are comfortable in their own skins, even when markedly different from the rest of the team.

— Deborah J. Swiss, *Women Breaking Through: Overcoming the Final 10 Obstacles at Work*

When you contribute from your heart and from your own special talents, there's no time for doubt, no time to worry about money, no time to get distracted by things that don't matter. You just know deep down that if you do what you're meant to do, you'll move ahead with full confidence and do the right thing.

— Elaine St. James, *Simplify Your Work Life*

> " Without skill, you are just a font of unfulfilled ideas.... Without passion, all the skill in the world won't lift you above craft. Without skill, all the passion in the world will leave you eager but floundering. Combining the two is the essence of the creative life. "

— Twlya Tharp, *The Creative Habit*

ATTITUDE

A constructive attitude is a prerequisite to any relationship, productive process, or profitable enterprise—like rain alternating with sunshine. You can learn, cultivate, improve, and strengthen a nurturing attitude. A great attitude grows from enthusiasm, meaning, and perspective. If your attitude suffers, it is time to step back, readjust, and reconsider. Attitude controls the variables that control your destiny.

LEGACY LADIES

* **Foolish are they indeed who trust to fortune!**
— Shikibu Murasaki

* **To a brave man, good and bad luck are like his right and left hand. He uses both.**
— Saint Catherine of Sienna

* **You just have to learn not to care about the dust mites under the beds.**
— Margaret Mead

* **I'm not happy, I'm cheerful. There's a difference. A happy woman has no cares. A cheerful woman has cares but has learned to deal with them.**
— Beverly Sills

This mini-collection represents our roots— wisdom many may have grown up with. These idea-seeds encourage genetic progression: if we share what we know, then we can prepare for storms. Gardens need to be resilient. (See this collection grow online.)

Strategic Cheerfulness

by Stephanie Medlock

Being cheerful is not a quality that shows up in any business's list of desirable attributes for prospective employees. It's not on Howard Gardiner's index of multiple intelligences (at least not specifically). When it is a manufactured emotion, such as the forced smile delivered by an airline stewardess to the drunken businessman who has patted her bottom, cheerfulness is actually harmful to a person's self esteem.

But cheerfulness is a fabulous quality that has a long-term benefit both on the individual who is cheerful and on everyone around her. Although this may never be measured, it has a huge impact on the bottom line of every business. Utilize cheerfulness as a way to:

- **Inspire progress.** Organizationally, the cheerful voice moves a group towards the successful conclusion of its task.

- **Encourage interaction and tolerance.** In customer service, when an irate customer meets someone who cheerfully promises to attend to the problem, it deflates anger.

- **Attract others.** The cheerful woman's office is the one easily filled with colleagues. She is often invited to meetings and functions, even if she does not absolutely need to be there, because a cheerful attitude is nourishing to others.

- **Motivate.** In crass financial terms, most organizations are in the process of making deals that create profit, product, or investor benefit. Those deals require the willingness of a group to work together, to act out their own desires within a framework of benevolent self interest, and to, at times, sacrifice their own wishes for the good of a project. Cheerfulness is the oil that soothes what can potentially be abrasive interactions.

- **Influence.** An individual who has a reputation for being cheerful is the person others go to for advice, volunteer to work with, and stay late with to finish a project. They are who you want on your team.

Ignore rules. In nearly every major scientific advance, the individual who changed an entire paradigm did not work in the discipline in which the advance was made. This meant that his or her imagination was not constrained by the rules of argument that dominated that discipline, and was free to combine what he or she knew of the field with other types of information.

STEPHANIE MEDLOCK

Ms. Medlock is Assistant Director of Professional Studies at the Graham School of General Studies at the University of Chicago. She develops new courses and certificates in emerging fields to help individuals change careers or enhance existing ones. Ms. Medlock developed the nationally known publishing certificates, including those in Medical Writing and Editing, and programs in nonprofit management, museum publishing, and translation studies. ■ Working first as a journalist for several east coast newspapers, Ms. Medlock earned a Masters of Arts in Social Sciences from the University of Chicago. She also worked in public relations for Zenith Corporation. International travel rounds out her perspective to recognize new and emerging trends in employment and nonprofit concerns. Ms. Medlock served on the Board of North West Indiana Literacy Project and has won several awards for her writing. She is also a gardener, a dancer, and a dreamer, lives in North Indiana and works in Chicago. Visit www.grahamschool.uchicago.edu.

Cheerfulness has a long-term benefit on the individual who is cheerful, on everyone around her, and makes a huge impact on the bottom line.

The Attitude of Gratitude

by Colette Baron-Reid

Gratitude is essential for well-being. Even the most difficult situations have something inherent in them to be grateful for. The 'attitude of gratitude' allows you to see value in everything: every situation, every part of life, every human being that crosses your path.

- **Gratitude allows you to recognize grace.** Be thankful for challenges, successes, even every seeming failure because each helps you grow and evolve with courage. You can't be grateful and fearful at the same time.

- **Gratitude is related to humility** and is the vehicle by which you can recognize what you can and cannot do yourself. When grateful, your ego is not running the show. Your spirit is aware of connectedness and recognizes you are one among many. To feel supported and to grow from your lessons enables you to acknowledge your wide-ranging gifts.

- **Review those things (big or small), at least twice a week, that contribute to your well being.** Gratitude is active. Relive your experiences. When you confront rejection, simply remember it is an opportunity to grow. When successful, remember you are a co-creator: nothing you ever do or accomplish is done alone.

- **Remind yourself that you are a 'work-in progress.'** Be grateful for the tools you have that enable you to make the appropriate amends and changes in yourself and your attitude.

COLETTE BARON-REID

Ms. Baron-Reid is an internationally renowned intuitive counselor with clients spanning over 21 countries. With a strict non-solicitation policy, Ms. Baron-Reid has attracted over 8,500 clients through word of mouth and referrals. Her unique service combines her extraordinary clairvoyant ability with her extensive psychology, spiritual science, and addiction recovery background. Ms. Baron-Reid describes herself as a "cosmic map reader and life story analyzer." She reveals where clients' life compasses are pointing, how to take responsibility for what they think, and helps them acknowledge the consequences attached to their actions. ■ Ms. Baron-Reid's other brilliant talent is as a published singer-song writer. She is signed to EMI music and records her own CD's. With regular columns in numerous papers and magazines, appearances on TV and radio, she was featured as one of six unique visionaries in the documentary feature film called "Hand of Fate." She is a regular speaker and has presented her intuitive development experiential workshop to full capacity groups in L.A., New York, Santa Fe, Park City, Vancouver, Toronto, and London. She lives in Toronto. Visit www.colettebaronreid.com. Author of **Remembering the Future**.

GERI BRIN

Brinsights LLC is a unique boutique marketing and communications company headed by Ms. Brin. She spent twenty three years at Fairchild Publications, most recently as Vice President of Publishing. Other positions she held were Executive Editor and Publisher of *HFN*, (the home furnishings trade weekly), Publisher and Editor in Chief of *Entrée*, (a gourmet housewares and food monthly), and senior fashion features editor of *WWD*. She also created and oversaw their Summit Program for five years. ■ Ms. Brin started Brinsights in 1998. They produce high-level symposiums, conceptualizes and develops custom publications, videos and web sites, and creates branding strategies to help clients market their products. ■ Working with accounts such as Sears Roebuck, American Express, *Seventeen Magazine*, *Fortune Magazine*, and The Children's Defense Fund, among others, Ms. Brin creates individual strategies for marketing to businesswomen. She works in New York, NY. Visit www.brinsights.com.

Gratitude Shouldn't Wait

by Geri Brin

How many times have you heard someone—following a life-threatening illness—say that she *now* was going to be grateful for every day she had and tell all her loved ones how much she cared? Gratitude shouldn't wait. We must say thanks every day for what we have *before* we're threatened at having it taken from us. Follow these daily guidelines to remind you of the special qualities and beauty you possess. Be grateful for:

- **opportunities and choices** presented to us and for those we make ourselves
- **people who do nice things**—no matter how small
- **those who teach us**—no matter how limited
- **simple pleasures**—even a smile from a stranger
- **acceptance by others**—even when we make a mistake
- **artists**—who create beauty for us to see and experience
- **musicians**—who create melodies for us to hear
- **children**—who run to hug us and have words to surprise
- **parents**—we can run to hug and tell us truths we need to hear
- **a friend**—we can call any time and always depend upon

- **health**—including well being, treatments, and solutions available
- **voices**—so we can speak out and express ideas
- **ears**—so we can listen to others and learn from them
- **spirit**—to rely upon, even when someone tries to dampen it
- **tastes**—of a gourmet meal or foods enjoyed at unexpected times
- **our bodies**—to perform and rise to challenges—a swimmer in a two-mile race in rough ocean waters, a marathon runner on a rainy day, a tennis player in the blistering heat
- **emotions**—to give us the ability to laugh or cry
- **the sun**—beginning or ending of each day, giving us the exquisite beauty of rising or setting.

For these we are grateful.

Say thanks every day for what you have before you're threatened at having it taken away.

When given the chance, women will make decisions based more on freedom, flexibility, and joy rather than their bank accounts. Some women do not feel that they have the luxury to think about their freedom, flexibility, and joy; they have to think about taking care of their children and paying the mortgage. [But] working for love and passion, with money as icing on the cake, is the ideal.

— Victoria Colligan and Beth Schoenfeldt,
Ladies Who Launch

When you bid for greater
power, you must, paradoxically,
have arrived at a state where
you do not personally care,
from an ego point of view,
whether you achieve it this time
or not. You must be prepared
to bid again and again until
you succeed.

— José and Lena Stevens, *The Power Path:
The Shaman's Way to Success in Business and Life*

> There are no happy jobs.
> There are only happy workers.
>
> — Joanne Gordon, *Be Happy at Work:*
> *100 Women Who Love Their Jobs, And Why*

Sometimes we get so busy pursuing our dream that we forget to notice the degree to which we're living it already. We compound our frustration by measuring our level of success or happiness against someone else's. We compare our insides to their outsides.

— Victoria Moran, *Creating a Charmed Life*

Underlying Assumptions of Four Generations:

- The Traditionalists (1928–1945): 'I want to join the world and benefit accordingly.'

- The Boomers (1946–1964): 'I want to help change the world— but I also need to compete to win.'

- The Generation X (1965–1979): 'I can't depend on institutions. I need to keep my options open.'

- The Generation Y (1980–2000): 'I need to live life now—and work toward long-term shared goals.'

— Tamara Erickson,
The Generation Y Guide to Thriving at Work

"

Recognition is key to learning, motivation, productivity, and sense of identity. Without it there can be no goals set and no sustained effort at a task. It is the motivational engine that allows you to develop the mastery required to pursue an ambition. Ambitions are at first the product and then, later, the source of this profoundly animating and defining response.

— Anna Fels, *Necessary Dreams: Ambition in Women's Changing Lives*

"

COMMUNICATION

If communication is fundamental to the human condition, why is poor communication responsible for almost all conflict? An ability with words can decrease conflict. Communication is an exploration, much like reading a map through a forest. It occurs best when each side values the messages of the others—both the topographer who creates the map and the traveler who reads it.

LEGACY LADIES

✳ **Why don't you write books people can *read*?**
— NORA JOYCE, TO HER HUSBAND, JAMES JOYCE

✳ **Language exerts hidden power, like the moon on the tides.**
— RITA MAE BROWN

✳ **It's useless to hold a person to anything he says while he's in love, drunk, or running for office.**
— SHIRLEY MACLAINE

✳ **One never discusses anything with anybody who can understand. One discusses things with people who *cannot* understand.**
— GERTRUDE STEIN

This mini-collection represents our roots— wisdom many may have grown up with. These idea-seeds encourage genetic progression: if we share what we know, then we can prepare for storms. Gardens need to be resilient. (See this collection grow online.)

The Wisdom of Inquiry

by Debi Davis

Men don't ask for directions; women don't ask questions. Oftentimes, out of fear of the possible response, women make assumptions rather than obtain facts. In some instances, assumptions can lead to heartache or, at the very least, misunderstandings. Sometimes through mis-assumptions, you lose things you deem important: friends, financial security . . . even marriage. Here are ways to avoid the risk of damaging assumptions:

- **Be careful of festering thoughts and false evaluations.** Ask yourself if you are making connections where there may not be any. If the premise for the conclusion is inaccurate, the conclusion drawn will also have no validity.

- **Recognize when you assume that those you care about must *know* what you want**, how you feel, or how you would want a situation handled. When the friend, business associate, or loved one doesn't perform as assumed, their lack of expected and anticipated action can then be misconstrued as thoughtlessness or lack of caring. In most cases, this assumption could not be further from the truth!

- **Ask questions of others' feelings.** Just because you may know a person well does not mean you know what they want.

- **State your feelings about anything you deem to be important.** This may mean that you run the risk of hearing something that you would prefer not to hear. But it is better to hear it and know where you stand than to let your concerns or assumptions fester, taking you down a false path that could lead to pain.

- **Clarify things that don't fit.** Go with your instincts. If something causes you to feel doubt in your dealings with another, speak up. Clarify the *real* situation rather than attempt to make puzzle parts fit all by yourself. Just because you may have a knack for reading people, this does not mean they have the same ability to read you.

Author of ***Weight Loss Through Visualization***, ***Back Off! I'll Lose Weight When I'm Ready***, ***Why Don't You Love Me? I'm the Best Choice***, ***Helpers***, ***A Practical Guide to Coping With a Loved One's Terminal Illness***, ***Beyond Atkins...The Hormone Diet***, and ***Wisdoms for a Better Life***

Developing skills of discernment will help you identify a genuine friend or partner, create acceptable boundaries, and avoid toxic human invaders. Your friendship is a gift. Discern with whom you share it!

DEBI DAVIS

Ms. Davis is the founder of Fit America, one of the fastest growing companies in the weight loss and wellness industry. In 1991, 85 pounds overweight and facing bankruptcy while raising two young children, Ms. Davis obtained funds to start her company by pledging her Rolex watch as collateral. Today, with her former husband, she directs the $46 million national company that features a physician-led and supported approach to weight management. Ms. Davis' success is a remarkable story of triumph over adversity. For three consecutive years, *Working Woman* magazine recognized Fit America as one of America's top 500 women-owned businesses. She and her company have been featured on *CNN* and other television pro-grams, as well as in *Success* magazine, *FSB* (*Fortune Small Business*), *Newsweek*, and *American Venture*. Her advice on weight loss is often featured in *Redbook* and *Bridal Guide*. Ms. Davis believes in giving back to her Florida community and is active in numerous civic organizations. She works in Deerfield Beach, FL. Visit www.fitamericamd.com.

DONNA FISHER

Ms. Fisher is a nationally known authority on the importance of people skills, clear communication, and the personal touch in today's busy, topsy-turvy world. She is an introvert who not only learned how to network, but then networked her way to entrepreneurial success. She is the president of both Donna Fisher Presents, a provider of keynotes and trainings for corporate meetings, conferences and conventions, and HiHat Inc., a manufacturing and retail business for drums and percussion instruments. She is also the founder and designer for Soft & Luxurious, custom designed and hand-crafted fashion accessories. ■ Ms. Fisher's books have been translated into five languages, recommended by *Time Magazine* and used as reference books in corporations and universities. She is a Certified Speaking Professional who speaks on the power of people communicating and connecting to create opportunities. She lives and works in Houston, TX. Visit www.donnafisher.com

Be accountable to someone. Speak of what you want to do and let others encourage you. It is easier to accept invitations than to create all the initiative by yourself.

Build a Support Network

by Donna Fisher

Few professionals become successful without making connections and receiving help from others. In fact, the most masterful networkers create magical results around them, and you never know they are networking! They make connecting a way of life:

- **Make a networking plan.** Determine what you have to offer and what you want from others. Who do you need in your support system? Find people that you can call on and count on.

- **Give up the 'Lone Ranger' mentality.** Power comes from *inter*dependence, not *in*dependence. Your network is only as strong as the relationships it's made of.

- **Graciously listen to others.** You connect through focused attention. Develop a childlike curiosity and you are less likely to be judgmental. Be delightfully interested and do not prejudge: deal with others through an open filter. Wonder why someone is different and you will uncover reasons you don't know.

- **Be both resourceful and generous when exchanging**

information. Give thoughts, ideas, contacts, suggestions, and encouragement. Practice contributing to every conversation. A thoughtful person is a remembered person.

- **Eliminate rejection.** If you feel rejected when asking for what you want, it is because of your approach. If you are seeking help from others to meet your goals, give information and strengthen relationships when contacting them by understanding their goals. If receiving a negative response, they aren't rejecting you personally; instead, turn the interaction into a benefit for both of you. They may be the wrong resource for what you need but can help point you in the right direction.

- **Accept opportunities.** The more you give, participate, and contribute, the more you will receive back.

Author of ***Power Networking, People Power, Power NetWeaving*** and ***Professional Networking for Dummies***.

Ask for what people can give you, not for what they can't.

Male speakers are most influential using a 'task-oriented style.' A 'social style' works best for women. When going into a negotiation, in addition to arming themselves with information, ideas, and resolve, women must also bring nonthreatening social mannerisms: cooperative, interested in the needs of others, and avoid being confrontational. This does not mean they need to back down or give in.

— Linda Babcock and Sara Laschever, *Women Don't Ask*

Individual thinking styles include: analytical, organized, expressive, and imaginative. Sometimes style differences can be dramatic, even damaging. The most creative and productive thinking results from exercising all four styles. Try looking at the situation with a new perspective or seek help from someone with an alternate style.

— Joanne G. Sujansky and John van Sprang,
The Keys to Conquering Change: 100 Tales of Success

"

If a woman in a position of authority talks in ways expected of women, she is more likely to be liked than respected. If she talks in ways expected of men, she is more likely to be respected than liked. It is ironic that the risk of losing likability is greater for women in authority, since evidence indicates that many women care so much about whether or not they are liked.

— Deborah Tannen, *Talking From 9 to 5*

"

Make listening to customers a regular discipline. Each day, discover something new by observing, eavesdropping, and paying attention to them. Also, make listening to customers a measurable requirement in every department. Create an inter-departmental task force to spread customer information. Call on input from experts in other fields who serve your customers.

— Mary Lou Quinlan, *Just Ask a Woman*

Foster community among your customers—they like to help one another with problems, tips, and to swap experiences. People like to contribute ideas and thoughts! Forums for dialogue makes them feel connected to your site. Those who voice an opinion online are going to return to see how others have reacted.

— Patricia Seybold, *Customers.com*

"

Move your team toward productive action by getting them to use the power of their communications— every ad, every speech, every retail outlet, every meeting, every press release, every customer meeting—as a chance to get your story out to the world.

— Sandra Spataro
and Keith Yamashita, *Unstuck*

"

WOMEN WHO WIN AT WORK • © 2009 Liane Sebastian

"

If an e-mail volley is more than three rounds, pick up the phone. If you're taking more than five minutes to compose a message, use the phone. A two-way conversation is the way two can solve issues twice as fast.

— Susan RoAne, *Face to Face*

A great thirty-second sound bite contains:
- the name of your business
- your main product or service
- the customer group that uses your product or service
- one benefit to those customers.

— Paula Peters, *The Ultimate Marketing Toolkit*

"

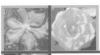

RELATIONSHIPS

To cultivate nurturing relationships, be flexible, tolerant, conscientious, able to compromise, and wise enough to honor differences. Relations germinate our greatest joys and our greatest sorrows, facilitate our greatest successes and accelerate our greatest setbacks. They demand the most from us. When we follow our hearts with wisdom, we find the best connections and symbiotic relations with other creatures sharing our life's gardens.

LEGACY LADIES

✳ **What I cannot love, I overlook.**
— ANAÏS NIN

✳ **You cannot belong to anyone else, until you belong to yourself.**
— PEARL BAILEY

✳ **We cannot do great things in life; we can only do small things with great love.**
— MOTHER TERESA

✳ **The bitterest tears shed over graves are for words left unsaid and deeds left undone.**
— HARRIET BEECHER STOWE

This mini-collection represents our roots— wisdom many may have grown up with. These idea-seeds encourage genetic progression: if we share what we know, then we can prepare for storms. Gardens need to be resilient. (See this collection grow online.)

Focus on the Goal

by C. Cie Armstead

To comfortably and effectively get along with someone else, remember your ultimate objectives for that specific relationship, and let that bigger-picture perspective govern your behavior. Recognize your primary goals for that particular interaction and respond accordingly. Then you can build strong relationships with full participation—both as a leader and as a contributor. For mutually rewarding relationships, ponder and practice these suggestions:

- **Begin within yourself**—Know and accept your strengths and those areas that require more development. Honestly assess your actions and motives. Give yourself constructive verbal and mental reinforcement. Choices must come from you or else you can get lost in others' priorities.

- **Use and nurture your strengths**—Use your gifts, particularly in service to others. As you accept the skills you don't have, be careful not to allow someone else's insecurities to cause you to underplay your strengths.

- **Balance leadership with humility**—Effective leaders know how to masterfully take the helm while humbly interacting with their team. This requires you to be secure in yourself to avoid feeling threatened by others' strengths.

- **Consider the other person**—Think about what he or she may want from the interaction. Strategically accommodate the other person's preferred mode of interacting while maintaining your own integrity. You may have to stretch and adapt outside of your comfort zone.

- **Examine your definitions**—Decide what success, failure, and similar life-governing terms mean for you. These terms imply a continuum that is more internal than external. Many relationships are severely damaged because one or both parties measure their relationship using inappropriate or different yardsticks.

- **Resist distractions**—During personal interactions, devote your full attention to the person. Sincerely listen if you want to be efficient.

- **Rise above the mire of insignificant detail**—Too often people hurt each other by squabbling over the inconsequential and hanging onto defunct positions. By focusing on the primary relationship goals, you can identify and disengage from debilitating detail.

- **Allow people to be human**—For the most part, all people do the best that they can at any given moment. Expect and accept that people will not be perfect. Extend kindness, forgiveness, and compassion whenever possible.

- **Use humor**—In strong relationships, both parties learn to laugh at many of the circumstances that could lead to arguments. Much of what people disagree about can actually serve as the source of comical relief when the focus returns to what's *really* important in the relationship.

Accommodate to others' styles without losing who you are. Recognize the positions and utilize the style of those with whom you deal.

C. CIE ARMSTEAD

Ms. Armstead has devoted her career to working with a wide variety of professionals, most notably as a managing editor for the American Bar Association. Coordinating volunteers, staff, and ABA management, Ms. Armstead is key in the creation of many successful publications. She currently serves as the Director of Diversity Initiatives and manages many successful interchanges between various divisions of the ABA and the community.  Striving striving for a life of service, Ms. Armstead has cultivated several other key roles that provide opportunities for building relationships. In August 1992, she married her best friend, and she serves alongside of him in his Evanston Illinois ministry. Ms. Armstead holds a Bachelor's degree in Journalism from Northwestern University, and a Masters degree in Public Administration/Nonprofit Management from Chicago's Roosevelt University. For more than 25 years, she has also been active in the fitness industry as a trainer, instructor, health club manager, business owner, wellness writer, and public speaker. In 1993, Ms. Armstead co-founded the African-American Association of Fitness Professionals, a nonprofit community service organization. She works in Chicago, IL. Visit www.abanet.org/diversity.

Achieve Rewarding Relationships

by Dr. Ellen Sherman

Whether our dream is to have a better relationship with a member of our family, a person at work, or a friend, certain strategies can assist. Here are a few that will help us achieve the relationship we want:

- **Focus on ourself.** Most of us mentally review what's bad about our relationships. We think about what someone did to us or said to us. But this rarely gets us anywhere and a better question to ask is: 'What can I do to improve this relationship?'

- **Stay positive.** It doesn't matter if we have a problem with work, family, friendship, or love. Our attitude toward people has a lot to do with the way people relate to us. Stay positive, neutral, and friendly when approaching another.

- **It's rarely personal.** Have we ever had someone respond in a negative way even when we approach them positively? This happens to all of us. If it happens, don't assume that we did or said something to cause their reaction. Take the approach that they're having a bad day. Let it go for another time or just walk away.

- **Distance toxic people.** Some people are just nasty. Such people will undermine our self-confidence and leave us doubting our own reality. Neutralizing people who contaminate our self-esteem means keeping them outside our inner circle. Know who they are. Avoid confiding in them or spending much time in their company.

ELLEN SHERMAN, PH.D.

Dr. Sherman is a licensed mental health professional in private practice. She received her Masters degree in marriage and family therapy at St. Thomas University and holds a Ph.D. in family therapy from Nova Southeastern University. She is active in several community organizations including the League of Women Voters, the National Council of Jewish Women, as well as serving as a Board Member of the Florida Association for Marriage & Family Therapists, and the Palm Beach Association for Marriage & Family Therapists. Dr. Sherman has taught at several South Florida colleges and universities, she voluntarily lectures to local community organizations on solving relationship and family problems. As a clinical member of the American Association for Marriage and Family Therapists and National Board for Certified Counselors, she lives and works in Boca Raton, Florida. Visit www.marriagefriendlytherapists.com/ellensherman.php

Focus on the present. Keep discussion to the subject and be alert for derailing techniques like changing subjects or diverting attention.

MARTHA BOSTON

Ms. Boston is an international trainer, coach, business consultant, and a lifelong student of the workings of the human heart, mind, and spirit. Founding Higher Ground in 1979, Ms. Boston helps organizations and individuals develop a deep appreciation for collaboration and teamwork. She teaches academic personal growth and professional development programs for organizations ranging from small nonprofits to Fortune 500 companies. She facilitates Insight Seminars with Interaction Associates. Through teaching at the University of Texas at Austin and the University of Houston at Clear Lake, she has developed a broad-based understanding of contemporary challenges. ■ With

degrees in government, law, and theology, Ms. Boston says that much of her best education comes from her clients and her dogs. She helps people find higher ground internationally with unique and impactful learning opportunities in settings ranging from boardrooms to mountaintops to sailing the high seas. She is "a recovering attorney," having won a case before the U.S. Supreme Court when only 29 years old. She lives and works in Austin, TX. Visit www.higherground.net.

Reveal Motivations

by Martha Boston

People are inspired to work together when their values are aligned. Projects are most efficient and profitable when everyone aims toward a common purpose. But often the participants can share the same goal, yet have both different values attached to it and different methods to achieve it. For successful collaboration, all motivations *need* to be known and articulated. Not addressing them can be the *main* source of conflict! Avoid by devising a process to reveal each participant's motivations:

- **Gauge commitment.** So often people *say* they are committed, but really are not. Other tasks always become more important to do. Slowly the project is sabotaged—sometimes deliberately and sometimes not—because the person hasn't answered the most fundamental question: 'What's in it for me?' This question drives *everyone*. If you were to ask even the most altruistic person why she does what she does, a Mother Theresa would answer honestly, 'because it feels good' or 'because God asked me to.'

- **Ask first why *you* want what you want.** What are you looking for in each experience? Such questions often stir up guilt because motivations can seem selfish. Yet personal stakes *always* underlie interest. Resolve and let go of any fear about self-inquiry! When you know what you want, you can also meet the needs of others who know what they want. It is hard to meet the needs of those who *don't* know what they want.

- **Determine what colleagues want, expect, and where each wants to go.** To best work with anyone, find out first what matters to them. Encourage them to *say* what they want. Ask a series of questions: 'What are you going to like about working on this project? If you buy into this strategy, what's the attraction? What might you learn, what skills might you use, what do you find appealing? What is *unappealing* about this project?' It will probably take four or five questions to gain an increased awareness of what they are thinking. If someone is just doing a job for the money, then know that. Accept the value diversity in the motivations you find. You may not approve, but if you accept, you can work from an accurate base. Maybe you can revamp the project to better address the needs of each participant.

- *Express* **what you want** *and* **what others want.** Do not allow motivations to remain hidden. Set up an environment where desires are requested, expressed, encouraged, promoted, and appreciated. Disclose motivations together. Keep discussions functional and these topics won't feel dangerous. Most people *want* to advance. Acknowledge that.

- **Work from strengths.** Motivations are rarely just about a paycheck. To make a valuable contribution is usually high in everyone's priority list.

By understanding each team member's motivation, you can align everyone together, move forward efficiently, and serve each contributor at a high level. Whatever discomfort there may be in revealing motivations is more than made up for in good decisions. Although uncomfortable, change is the only way to progress. Hopefully, the inquiry first happening behind closed office doors will migrate out into conference rooms, and finally accepted differences can become more mainstream.

Be specific about your goals and expectations. Don't assume that others know what you're thinking. They can't read your mind.

— Dr. Donna Brooks and Lynn Brooks,
Ten Secrets of Successful Men that Women Want to Know

Talking about subjects rather than about yourself earns the perception that you're a thoughtful, intelligent, mature person worth listening to. Focus on issues instead of people.

— Phyllis Mindell, Ed.D., *How to Say It for Women*

Each couple has to have a plan, and both partners have to know what the plan is and what their responsibilities are. Successfully managing finances together requires honesty, communication, flexibility, compromise, and a good dose of love and patience—indeed, the very qualities that make for a good relationship.

— Harriet Pappenheim and Ginny Graves,
Bringing Home the Bacon

"Conflict provides an opportunity for growth, to enrich a relationship. The opposite of love is apathy, not hate. As long as there is conflict, there is energy to work on it. Once apathy has set in, it may be too late.

— Ruth Herrman Siress,
Working Woman's Communications Survival Guide

No matter how much you do for your company's bottom line, if you complain or have difficulty getting along with people, you will undermine your efforts. Attitude is more important than skills; skills can be more easily taught than attitudes."

— Debra Fine, *The Big Talk*

"Technology is not a substitute for face-to-face contact. To motivate employees, you must know and be able to read them. Trust requires that you build a relationship with as many of your direct reports and their direct reports as possible.

— Kay Hammer, *Work Place Warrior*

Focus on the customer—not on you, your business, your employees, or anything else. What customers *do* care about is how all these matters affect them.

— Susan F. Benjamin,
Instant Marketing for Almost Free

> Stop networking. Why? There are better ways to meet people. Business is personal. The best way to meet someone is through a referral. Additionally:
>
> 1. Do what you enjoy.
> 2. Build with one person at a time.
> 3. Make a Good People to Know list and stay in touch.
> 4. Cultivate your VIPs—with a maximum of 20 people.
> 5. Nurture your inner circle—friends and family who love you for who you are.

— Stephanie Palmer, *Good in a Room*

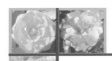

RESOLVE

Being a woman in business can often serve as an advantage. The best strategies for growth use the resources we have and help us develop more. By using feminine strengths, we can disarm, charm, or take the sting out of harsh messages. Success takes more than intelligence, talent, or skill. Resolve is the vow to find or create the right conditions to flourish—to withstand storms, droughts, floods, or conflict.

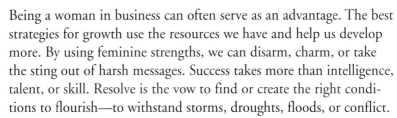

LEGACY LADIES

✳ **Life's under no obligation to give us what we expect.** —MARGARET MITCHELL

✳ **It takes as much courage to have tried and failed as it does to have tried and succeeded.** — ANNE MORROW LINDBERGH

✳ **If I had to live my life again, I'd make the same mistakes, only sooner.** — TALLULAH BANKHEAD

✳ **When you realize the value of all life, you dwell less on what is past and concentrate more on the preservation of the future.** — DIAN FOSSEY

This mini-collection represents our roots—wisdom many may have grown up with. These idea-seeds encourage genetic progression: if we share what we know, then we can prepare for storms. Gardens need to be resilient. (See this collection grow online.)

Make Better Decisions

by Julie Garella

Skills used in building a business need to evolve *especially* after reaching a certain success level. Enrich your decision-making abilities and confront any tendencies that may limit your effectiveness:

- **Act on research, not on emotion.** Women tend to gather information and form an opinion based on what they believe to be consensus. Most likely, the sources you tap are those advisors who know you, and understand your comfort levels. They edit their recommendations based on their knowledge of your behavior: they usually tell you what you want to hear. Additionally, like the terminally ill patient who continues to search for the doctor who holds out hope, it's easy to fall into the trap of hearing only the answer you were looking for. Make sure your research stretches your network resources and includes disinterested third parties who can lend objectivity to your decision making process.

- **Avoid paralysis of analysis.** If you've done the homework and received the information, *now act on it*! Too often you may tell yourself that you shouldn't do anything now. But when you've determined the best next steps, don't let your fears or anxieties take control of your moves! Use logic and sound business principles as your guides. Remember: while you're paralyzed, thinking about what to do, someone else is out there doing it!

- **Perfect is the enemy of very good.** Nothing is *ever* perfect! In business, as in nature, the most wonderful things often arise because of slight imperfections. Perfectionism holds women back—you get stuck on a single solution path. Recognize there is no one right answer, but many.

- **Have a Plan B.** Always! Learn how to see alternatives and opportunities. Ask for help. Even include a Plan C in reserve!

- **Accept what works.** There are tried-and-true methodologies for growing businesses. Don't waste time and energy trying to reinvent the wheel. Learn the rules. Find 'translators' and experts who can bridge the gap between you and the financial world. These helpers can shortcut your learning process. In business, men *do* ask for directions—by hiring advisors!

A *lot* of psychology goes into growing a business! How you make decisions determines whether you can advance to the majors or stay in the minor leagues.

Author of **Capitalize on Your Success**

Julie Garella

Providing strategic advisory services to businesses owned and operated by women, Ms. Garella utilizes her banking background to serve civic needs. ■ She began her career in financial services at Smith Barney Harris Upham in 1987 on the retail side and then for Interstate/Johnson Lane before founding Carnegie Capital Advisors, the Carolina's only SEC-registered women-owned investment management firm. In 1999, Ms. Garella launched Fairview Capital Ventures, LLC, an investment banking/venture capital firm focused on seed-stage and first-round capital, buyouts, and acquisitions for companies in the Southeast.

Together with partner Hugh McColl, the former chairman of the Bank of America, Ms. Garella had co-founded McColl Garella, an investment banking firm. Since, she has re-joined Smith Barney in March 2006 as Director of Business Development for Citigroup Capital Strategies. ■ Ms. Garella serves on several boards including: Women's Leadership Exchange, United Way's Women's Leadership Initiative, Women's Impact Fund Presbyterian, and Center for Women's Business Research. She lives and works in New York, NY. www.citigroupcapitalstrategies.com.

MELISSA WAHL

Ms. Wahl is with the Women President Organization in New York and was formerly with Outreach for Women's American ORT, both national nonprofit philanthropic organizations supporting women in business. Prior, she served as Executive Director of the National Association for Female Executives and Publisher of *Executive Female* magazine. She also served as Director of AMIT Women. ■ Ms. Wahl's expertise in women's workplace issues is utilized as a frequent resource for many national publications, including *The Wall Street Journal*, *The New York Times*, and the *Washington Post*. ■ Ms. Wahl is a Judge for the National Women's Hall of Fame and was formerly a Board member of the New York Women's Agenda. ■ A certified association executive, Ms. Wahl has over eleven years of management experience in both for-profit and not-for-profit associations. She is also a dedicated volunteer and has served as Chair of the Center for Association Executives Career Enrichment Program. For the New York Society of Association Executives, she has served as Chair of the Professional Development Committee, Chair of the Awards & Recognition Committee, and now sits on their Board of Directors. ■ Ms. Wahl lives in New York, NY, with her husband and is the mother of two sons. See www.womenpresidentsorg.com.

Self Foundation

by Melissa Wahl

The good-girl approach is not getting us where we want to go. Women are not as assertive or as likely to self-promote as are our male counterparts. We don't want to brag or talk too much about ourselves. This holds us back. If we can't step up to the plate, we will never have the opportunity to hit a ball. *Each* professional woman must learn to play the networking game—by first establishing who *she* is to give her the courage to extend herself. Here are considerations to increase networking our strength:

- **Women become discouraged and then give up too easily.** The Queen of Cold Calling is Wendy Weiss. She proves that to reach someone, to sell them something, or even to tell them about an opportunity, it takes about seven tries! Most women give up after two or three.

- **Determine our assets.** What can we exchange with someone for the help we need? For example, explore promotional possibilities. Or even just contribute *time*. Every group needs something done, even if just stuffing envelopes and attaching stamps. Women often undervalue *time* as a contribution. Be sure to have assets for bartering when asking others for help.

- **Define who we are.** We identify ourselves with our jobs. But we are the sum of *all* the great things we do. Churchill said: 'Live not by what you do, but by what you give.'

- **Mentor another** (woman *or* man). Help another professional get a leg up, avoid the land mines, and obtain recognition. If we don't have someone to mentor through our job, we can seek someone through participation in an organization. A mentoree can inspire us to be sharp and to best utilize our contacts.

- **Show up.** Women are inhibited by vulnerability. It can be hard to walk into a room of strangers and have to put on a smile. The best strategy is to approach someone else standing alone who *also* had to walk in and put on a smile.

- **Speak and write articles** to connect with the local media. Investigate what coverage can be utilized. Let someone else do the bragging!

Openness to flexible work arrangements requires new productivity measurements and tools, new ways to determine success. Results matter more than where or how many hours are invested.

Resilient people believe they can directly influence the events that occur in their lives and translate their beliefs into actions. People who take charge over the aspects of their lives that are controllable thrive despite real-life problems and difficulties. And they are more likely to see change as an opportunity for growth rather than as a stressor.

— Karen Reivich and Andrew Shatté,
The Resilience Factor

Unstoppable people are your greatest resources, and are usually more than happy to talk about what they've learned. Welcome input from multiple perspectives. Value experience above everything else, and do not take advice from someone who hasn't created the results you want to achieve.

— Cynthia Kersey, *Unstoppable Woman*

"

The person who has built on her wins has mastered the art of training, strategy, and getting the right people in her corner. She forms fight plans and sticks with them. After every risky close call, she takes time to honestly evaluate the win. A *narrow* win affords us a sterling opportunity. Not only do we get the satisfaction of winning, but the chance to reevaluate and improve ourselves for the next bout.

— Jackie Kallen, *Hit Me with Your Best Shot*

"

Women tend to volunteer as a way of helping because we want to show that we have a variety of talents. But taking on any job without obtaining the proper authority wastes time as well as emotional and intellectual energy, creates confusion, unhappiness, and trouble. Offer your services *only* when you are certain that the task is a career opportunity.

— Gail Evans, *Play Like a Man, Win Like a Woman*

> The closest we can come to making the business world fair is to stand on our own two feet and defend ourselves or our ideas aggressively. We cannot expect others to defend us. We have to do that job ourselves. We expect leaders to respond to attacks, to set clear limits, and to defend themselves and their positions—on their own.

— Beth Gottfried and Anthony Parinello,
10 Secrets I Learned from the Apprentice

Leadership in time management requires you to: (1) figure out what matters most, (2) empower yourself and others to accomplish those important objectives, (3) remove obstacles to their accomplishment, and (4) eliminate procrastination. Ask, 'what ideas, projects, and programs—if implemented now—would significantly impact the profitability or productivity of my staff or organization?'

— Laura Stack, *Leave the Office Earlier*

Winners have no where to go but down. Arrogance and the trappings that come with winning cause myopia, and management loses sight of what's really happening with customers and in the marketplace. When you're winning, it's difficult to embrace change. Companies that think like an underdog, no matter how well they are doing, are able to keep their edge, and continually re-think their products or approach to the marketplace.

— Denise Shiffman, *The Age of Engage*

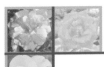

DISCIPLINE

Businesses and careers, like gardens, cannot thrive without the regular maintenance demanded by variable seasons and conditions. Discipline organizes chores and gives direction to daily activities. It transforms "have to's" and "shoulds" into preferences, especially when results become payoffs. Through diligence, we can dedicate ourselves to do what is necessary for each plant to thrive and each investment to mature.

LEGACY LADIES

✳ **Nothing that is worthwhile is ever easy.**
— INDIRA GANDHI

✳ **The pain of discipline is short,**
but the glory of the fruition is eternal.
— HARRIET BEECHER STOWE

✳ **I don't know that there are any**
short cuts to doing a good job.
— SANDRA DAY O'CONNOR

✳ **There is no time for cut-and-dried monotony.**
There is time for work. And time for love.
That leaves no other time!
— COCO CHANEL

This mini-collection represents our roots— wisdom many may have grown up with. These idea-seeds encourage genetic progression: if we share what we know, then we can prepare for storms. Gardens need to be resilient. (See this collection grow online.)

Chip Through Emotional Roadblocks

by Lucy Rosen

Each of us is our own biggest challenge. We throw more roadblocks in our own way than really exist! To best handle these, first recognize that self-made blocks do exist. Pragmatic roadblocks are often used as excuses for emotional ones. With a lack of funding, we can't get started. With a lack of childcare, we can't follow up on opportunities, etc. *Emotional* barriers (although primarily unnecessary) are the *really* difficult ones to grow beyond! First, we must differentiate real issues from emotional fears. Then, we must break through our emotional blocks:

- **Invest in ourself.** Get a business consultant. See a good therapist. Women use the financial excuse for not getting these kinds of assistance. We do not spend money on our businesses the way we do on ourselves, our families, or our houses. A woman might spend $5,000 on a new kitchen floor but balk at spending $5,000 on a business plan or $8,000 on a corporate identity that can really help build our businesses!

- **Determine emotional needs so they don't cloud decision-making.** Transfer skills. Women work very hard. We are creative, smart, and clever, but don't use this shrewdness enough in business. We are afraid of being called a bitch or of being called aggressive (rather than assertive). Most of all, we are afraid of not being *liked*. Women want to be liked more than *anything* else! We volunteer for *more* activities, sit on *more* boards, take on *more* and *more* responsibilities—all to be liked. Further, we think because we are *really* busy, we are valued. But are we doing the *right* things?

- **Seek recognition.** All people want to receive appreciation for their work. But women often don't speak up and *ask* for the pats on the back they need. Entrepreneurs with small staffs can become insulated and not receive the recognition they need. Often they look for recognition in less than optimal places. For example, many form personal friendships with employees. This is a really bad idea. It is hard to get mad at them. It makes business decisions more complicated.

- **Do not run your business like a family.** This is a common mistake for women! Business people without children are more susceptible to develop family-like relationships with colleagues. Remember that employees and clients come and go. Hopefully family members do not. Make an emotional separation between these two worlds. We must *care* about clients, but know the difference between them and family. This fine line between personal and professional emotional fulfillment should not be crossed. It is guaranteed to affect decision-making, not always to the benefit of our businesses.

- **Give validation.** We need it for ourselves and can often forget that others need it too. Remember to say 'thank you' and 'good job.' Every action causes a reaction. Be conscious, especially with employees, that the small things said can make a big difference. Employees tend to magnify and mirror our actions. Small things that we do for clients are remembered.

We must make investments in ourselves. Get a business consultant. See a therapist. Women too often use the financial excuse for not getting this kind of assistance.

LUCY ROSEN

Ms. Rosen is a visionary marketing, public relations, and business development professional. She is also the founder and president of Women on the Fast Track, an international networking organization for businesswomen. ■ As a successful entrepreneur, Ms. Rosen helps organizations grow with unique campaigns or image enhancement programs. Her clients have included major pharmaceutical companies, medical centers, hospitals, and not-for-profit organizations. Ms. Rosen serves as the Facilitator of the Long Island Chapter of the Women Presidents' Organization and is an advisory board member of PULSE. She has been a mentor and member of the U.S. Small Business Administration Advisory Services Department for Women in Business Program, and has taught for the American Women's Economic Development Corporation. She has also served on the Board of Directors of the New York City chapter of the National Association of Women Business Owners.

■ Ms. Rosen has made serving community causes an important part of her career. She annually donates a full year of her services to a chosen local not-for-profit group. ■ The author of a series of business "how-to" booklets, Ms. Rosen is based in New York and speaks nationally. Visit www.womenforhire.com and www.thebusinessdevelopmentgroup.com

LINDA L. LISTROM

Ms. Listrom is a senior partner at Jenner & Block, a major national law firm. She is Chair of the Firm's Litigation Committee and Co-Chair of its Defense and Aerospace Practice. Ms. Listrom specializes in complex business litigation and frequently litigates significant cases involving allegations of breach of contract and fraud. She regularly serves as lead trial counsel f o r General Dynamics Corporation, one of the firm's major clients involving a multi-billion dollar lawsuit against the United States Government.

Ms. Listrom is a member of the American Bar Association and its Section of Litigation; she co-chairs the Section's Trial Practice Committee and has served on several task forces for the Section. She lives and works in Chicago, IL. Visit www.jenner.com.

Giving people choices makes them happier and helps them form and maintain better relationships. It is good for business.

Play the Game

by Linda Listrom

The journey combining business, career, and family *always* involves two steps forward and one step back! Business has defined rules that must be considered against personal needs. Success means making the rules work *for* you rather than against you:

- **Factor the direction and level of your challenges.** Professional women face varying career decisions at defined points. For example, in the law firm there is a big difference between being an associate and being a partner. It is harder for an associate to be a mother; partnership makes delegation easier. However, partners have more client responsibilities that demand *your* attention and no one else's. Associates have the freedom to fill in for each other. Find colleagues at your level to best exchange advice, ideas, and often assistance.

- **Learn to generate business.** Intrinsically, service businesses are not very hospitable environments for women because of their time demands. Women with children struggle to come up with billable hours. Instead, find other ways to contribute where you can demonstrate value without putting in a disproportionate amount of time. Bring assistance to the company without needing to bring hours. Develop business either by cultivating new clients or by expanding current contacts. Important client relationships can take the heat off of time accounting and allow greater flexibility. At the beginning of her career, a young professional should think about how she'll bring in business. In the short run, such foundation-building requires *more* effort and *more* time. But ultimately, breaking out of the day labor category pays off. Also learn to make money from what others can do; this way you can create greater leverage and best optimize your resources.

- **Monitor networking habits.** To do a great job is important, but it won't get you to success. You also have to develop relationships with those who can nurture your career. *Consciously* work on your network! It is counterproductive to worry about rejection and easy to be paralyzed by fear. Following up on opportunities once initiated is the *most* difficult! Form a *strategy* of developing relationships that is consistent and open. Cultivate relationships with a variety of people and keep track of them. Maintain regular contacts such as with classmates, associates, etc. You never know which ones will lead to opportunity and which ones won't. Play the percentages. Networking is full of surprises! Often luck determines what happens, but you have to *be* there for luck to happen! Most people need to *push* themselves to build relationships both within and without their organizations. This can and must be done—and even be enjoyed! The surprises make it fun. Because relationship building is so unpredictable, it has to be nurtured over time to gain full benefit.

- **Maintain financial independence.** If a young woman learns only *one* thing, it should be how to take care of herself. If you can support yourself, you can withstand whatever happens in life, such as a divorce or widowhood. Self-sufficiency is axiomatic.

Often luck determines what happens,
but you have to be there for luck to happen!

Set up a schedule to review your financial dealings no less than once each quarter. Verify that your investment accounts, insurance policies, and estate plans are functioning as they should; make any necessary adjustments.

— Bambi Holzer,
Set for Life: Financial Peace for People Over 50

Two important functions of a leader are to offer a concrete definition of business reality and to say 'thank you.'

— Rosanne Badowski, *Managing Up: How to Forge an Effective Relationship with Those Above You*

"

Strive for 80% perfection. The difference between 80% and 100% won't be noticed by most people but will buy you more time to shift to other important tasks.

— Lois P. Frankel, *Nice Girls Don't Get the Corner Office*

The more energy we devote to multitasking, the less ability we have to refresh ourselves. Being fully engaged with the moment is the best way to relieve stress. Avoid multitasking to build a less grinding rhythm.

— Sally Helgesen, *Thriving in 24/7*

"

Seven Habits of Highly Effective Homepreneurs:

1. Get a routine.
2. Mark your territory.
3. Pimp your virtual office.
4. Stay on top of administrata.
5. Press the flesh— don't be isolated.
6. Work the web.
7. Keep your resume and portfolio current.

— Michelle Goodman, *The Anti 9 to 5 Guide*

"

If you continue to return to your daily process (whatever that may be), your creativity will burst forth in all sorts of unforeseen ways. You learn to be in the present, wait for ideas, appreciate your daily life, and feel the adventure you are living now (not when you are famous, successful, or dead). You learn that the struggle— quiet and small as it is—is really the greatest reward of all.

— Carol Lloyd, *Creating a Life Worth Living*

"

Six Big Traps to Avoid:

1. Being overly concerned with your image.
2. Spending too much on equipment and infrastructure.
3. Over-servicing clients and under-valuing your product or service.
4. Treating your business too much like a family.
5. Relying too heavily on 'experts.'
6. Failing to address weaknesses:
   a. Lack of planning.
   b. Lack of experience.
   c. Lack of management skill.
   d. Lack of promotion.

— Karin Abarbanel, *How to Succeed on Your Own*

PERSISTENCE

Plans and conversation are meaningless unless they provide the structure and content to continually inspire our mission. Without conviction, persistence becomes possible. Without persistence, like plants, plans cannot grow to fruition because the first storm will uproot any untended saplings. Often we need to support our perennial seedlings with stakes and fences to give them the tenacity to thrive from season to season.

LEGACY LADIES

✳ **When you come to a roadblock, take a detour.**
— Mary Kay Ash

✳ **It's by endurance that one gains rewards and comfort for one's pains.**
— Christine de Pisan

✳ **The worth of every conviction consists precisely in the steadfastness with which it is held.**
— Jane Addams

✳ **Never doubt that a small group of thoughtful, committed citizens can change the world. Indeed, it's the only thing that ever has.**
— Margaret Mead

This mini-collection represents our roots—wisdom many may have grown up with. These idea-seeds encourage genetic progression: if we share what we know, then we can prepare for storms. Gardens need to be resilient. (See this collection grow online.)

From Overwhelmed to Inspired

by Suzanne Falter-Barns

Every professional woman faces mountains of opportunities and has baskets of things to do. Most feel overwhelmed by myriad activities: handling investors, dealers, agents, critics, publishers, managers, directors, customers, employees, families, etc. How can one person be *everywhere* and do *everything*? How can you sustain, connect, and promote most effectively without going nuts? Work expands. But feeling overwhelmed is really a symptom of fearing failure! Not 'having time' can be an excuse not to pursue your dreams. If you feel overwhelmed:

- **Have patience.** Don't expect development to be fast. To create a niche *especially* takes time! In a culture of instant information, professionals quickly jump from promotion to promotion, from business to business. A mindset develops that demands fast results, and if they don't come, you must be doing something wrong, have an unappreciative boss, or bemoan your lack of a trust fund. But you *can't* speed up the development time required for living your dream! This process still moves at the same speed it always has. People need to be grounded in reality: *everything* can't be done at a greater speed!

- **Make partnerships.** Men tend to be competitive—to want to *beat* the other guy. Women are more prone to work collaboratively. This is an advantage. And the Internet is a *great* partnering tool that women tend to 'get.'

- **Research the gatekeepers in your field.** Locate professional organizations and resources for how to best approach decision-makers.

Learn whatever etiquette may be required. Get the education you need.

- **Develop systems.** Learn automation tools and techniques. There are great processes available—such as scheduling software packages. Take the time to learn them to save considerable time later!

- **Exploit communication technology.** Learn to work with people in other places. Although alone in a room, you can still have action and contact to people in a great number of places! Develop skills, for technology also provides new ways to be isolated; e-mail can be very effective but can't take the place of human contact. Maintain your Web site and continually make sure it is user-friendly.

- **Keep your fires stoked from those who receive your work.** Encourage feedback and ways to interact with audiences.

- **Publish electronically.** Don't wait for publishers to catch up to digital publishing opportunities. Although publishers *do* provide credibility and distribution, the Internet offers many other supportive avenues for promotion and visibility. Make your work available, and find partnerships with other sites.

- **Be satisfied with doing a little.** Doing a little is better than doing nothing. Rather than be intimidated by a mountain of work, choose to do the easiest part. This will help you establish a momentum.

- **Dive into your goal with abandon.** Commitment *does* get results. Although you may not receive what you expect for your effort, you're *not* going to get nothing!

SUZANNE FALTER-BARNS

Ms. Falter-Barns is a former corporate drone who reinvented her life and became a popular motivational writer and speaker. Her e-zine, *The Joy Letter*, is read by more than 2,500 people worldwide. She teaches teleclasses and leads retreats on creativity, writing, and how to live your dreams in workshops across the U.S. and Canada. She was a regular columnist for *New Age Journal*, and has written essays and articles for *The New York Times, SELF, Fitness, New Woman, Prevention, Cosmo Girl, More*, and *Parent*.

■ Ms. Falter-Barns taught creative writing at New York University, and appears as a cabaret singer and performer. ■ Her work helps readers reignite their creative sparks and stamp out the energy drains that get in the way of creative, joyful living. She lives and works in Essex, NY. Visit www.howmuchjoy.com.

Author of: ***Living Your Joy: A Practical Guide to Happiness***; ***How Much Joy Can You Stand? A Creative Guide to Facing Your Fears and Making Your Dreams Come True***; and ***Doin' the Box Step***, a novel.

SUZANNE PEASE

Starting her company in 1985, Ms. Pease first offered freelance illustration and soon discovered a niche in architectural renderings for planning boards and advertising. In 1990, Ampersand Graphics expanded to other areas of corporate identity management and brochure development. ■ As recent president of the National Association of Women Business Owners, Ms. Pease sits on many advisory boards and councils including the AOL Time Warner Small Business Advisory and the Wyndham Women on Their Way Advisory Board. She speaks widely for organizations around the country. ■ Ms. Pease believes that economic empowerment for women can solve many of the world's problems. Volunteer positions have developed her as a leader and introduced her to thousands of dynamic people. ■ She has won many awards including the New Jersey Women in Business Advocate– Small Business Administration and the Athena Award, Western Monmouth Chamber of Commerce. She has served as a NJ Elected Delegate to the White House Conference on Small Business. ■ Ms. Pease works in Morganville, NJ. Visit www.ampersandgraphics.com.

Perseverance Pays

by Suzanne Pease

Opportunities are created by participation! Put yourself in a place where your business can grow. Pursue the best contacts or information as an investment in your future. If you make cheap choices, you *seem* less successful, which then attracts less new business—a self-fulfilling prophecy. Here are ways to participate and persevere most optimally for business growth:

- **Maintain a viewpoint of fullness.** Recognize tools, communications, equipment, and/or promotions that can lead to new contacts. Utilize what you *have* versus waste time longing for what you don't have!

- **Spend the time and the money to attend appropriate events.** For example, a bus company owner spent $800 to attend a conference run by Toyota, even though she felt she couldn't afford it. While there, she secured a contract that more than paid for her trip! Be aware, though, that most pay-offs are not this immediate.

- **Have realistic expectations.** The return on networking and marketing efforts takes about three years to be realized. Three years seems to be the magic number to judge the viability of a new business or to gauge the payback for participating in an organization. Only then can you evaluate both what effort you put *into* your participation with what you have gotten out of it. It is either worth it after three years, or you can't sustain the commitment.

- **Form an economic foundation *before* starting a business.** Don't expect to put food on the table *and* grow a new venture for at *least* three years. Take care of your basic needs before taking on excessive risk.

- **Decipher *your* direction from other people's expectations.** If you feel that you *have* to live up to other's ideas, it can push you in directions you would not go on your own—both good and bad. If you have committed to a venture, make sure to have people around you that support you during days of self-doubt.

- **Craft business to your needs.** The workplace *is* becoming more flexible. However, an entrepreneur can have a successful business and not be a successful person. To be a successful person, you must be selfish and put your needs on the table. Carefully think through your priorities and choices. A successful business can create unhappy workers because choices are made without fully examining all of the ramifications.

- **Define how you present yourself.** For example, there is a perceptual difference between introducing yourself as a freelancer versus as a firm owner.

- **Temper expectations.** Most entrepreneurs start a business because they want freedom, wealth, and independence. But most entrepreneurs have to reinvest *most* of their profits for the first few years back into the business and put in 12-hour days! Those who want time for friends and family *and* hobbies need to look at the consequences of each choice.

- **Develop a long-term view.** Those that only *try* for a while in business don't make it through the twists, turns, and compromises needed to survive. Those in it for the long term are the ones who will make it.

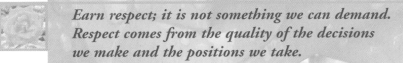

Earn respect; it is not something we can demand. Respect comes from the quality of the decisions we make and the positions we take.

The quality of our lives is determined more by how we respond to changes and tough situations than the situations themselves. Our best responses come from our inner strengths— flexibility and resiliency. The disruption of order is not only normal, it is where breakthroughs come.

— Marion Luna Brem,
The Seven Great Truths about Successful Women

If an idea is a good one, more than one person will have it. Don't freak out! Consider it a marketplace validation of your concept. Win through superior execution. It's not about being first, but about lasting. The key to success is not to be obsessed by rivals, or reactive to their moves. Stay focused on what you need to achieve.

— Robin Wolaner, *Naked in the Boardroom*

> If you can make the mental shift that allows you to see your competitors as both competitors *and* potential prospects, you put yourself in the right mindset to win.

— Ronna Lichtenberg, *Pitch Like a Girl*

> Think of business success as a process, not as something that happens overnight. Create a monthly strategy, weekly goals, and a daily action plan to build momentum.

— Marcia Rosen, *The Woman's Business Therapist*

Fight for yourself. Women *are* the fiercer sex. Nearly every Greek god of war is named after a goddess! Women fighters are most often motivated by revenge: righting a wrong, saving a reputation, defending the dead. But energy is better spent fighting *for* something tangible for yourself, like the freedom to do important work. To fight for your aims is not selfish.

— Harriet Rubin,
The Princessa: Machiavelli for Women

WOMEN WHO WIN AT WORK • © 2009 Liane Sebastian

If you want something better for your life and career, you owe it to yourself to go for it or reject it outright. Don't leave the dream dangling as a reminder of what you don't have the time, courage, or enthusiasm to grab. Do it or forget it.

— Vickie L. Milazzo, *Inside Every Woman*

We must always work smarter, think better, manage more humanely, and be more patient than our male counterparts. This is the price we pay for joining their club. If we maintain our female superiority, we can govern a much happier place than any man can.

— Nina DiSesa, *Seducing the Boys Club*

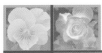

POTENTIAL

Potential exists in every situation. It combines knowledge, skills, perceptions, and aspirations to harvest opportunity. Use change to advantage by exploring multiple possibilities and developing a flexible skill set. Personal mastery over change occurs when we direct attention towards the potential we see—when we can bring to fruition what we have planted and nurtured.

LEGACY LADIES

✳ **Love dies only when growth stops.**
— PEARL S. BUCK

✳ **To keep a lamp burning, we have to keep putting oil in it.**
— MOTHER TERESA

✳ **Full maturity is achieved by realizing that you have choices to make.**
— ANGELA BARRON MCBRIDE

✳ **Women want men, careers, children, friends, luxury, comfort, independence, freedom, respect, love, and $3 pantihose that won't run.**
— PHYLLIS DILLER

This mini-collection represents our roots—wisdom many may have grown up with. These idea-seeds encourage genetic progression: if we share what we know, then we can prepare for storms. Gardens need to be resilient. (See this collection grow online.)

Fix Fatal Flaws

by Martha Barletta

The rules of business culture promote male gender qualities. For women to compete, we must understand these rules while we find ways to best contribute. And for all businesses to succeed, we must both temper and enhance the strengths of the male-dominated culture with those of the female. Here are suggestions to best navigate:

- **Learn self-control.** Women are more emotional and it hurts us in business. *Never* express negative emotions at work! Most emotions *don't* belong in the work place. Often we express frustration, anger, discouragement, or disappointment. Men don't know how to respond to these negatives—in fact no one does. But men also view these expressions as signs of weakness. Anger *never* allows for good judgement. Even though we may feel justified, we *always* regret it later and it *always* costs us. Though women are programmed to be more in touch with emotions, this doesn't mean we must *express* them! Research, (such as Daniel Goleman's on emotional intelligence) proves that expressing anger is not necessarily healthy. Often, it *increases* the anger. Better to dissipate it—to become distracted. Keep negative perceptions or emotions out of the office and express them to your friends instead.

- **Behave the way the culture understands.** To be effective, first conform to male customs. The workplace will not accommodate us; we must accommodate it. Imagine going on a foreign assignment, sent to Beijing. Maybe the office has five or six other Americans. We can't expect the Chinese to change to American ways for these five or six Americans!

But understanding *does* need to be created. Sometimes we must explain how we may act differently than expected, why our different approach can add value, and how it can often be better than conventional male behavior—especially in this new, decentralized Information Economy.

- **Allow for differences in gender culture.** Women evaluate the way men behave using female culture criteria and often take offense to what men don't mean to be offensive. For example, men like to banter and joke. But when teased, women feel put down or treated like outsiders. Men actually show that they *like* us when they tease! Because so many women react badly, men walk on eggshells around them.

- **Encourage new judgement criteria.** Many women miss being promoted because their skills are not recognized by male cultural definitions, even though they may be the best candidates. Men won't come to realize on their own how women offer new valuable skill ranges. We have to *show* them at the same time we learn to work *with* them. As a service to humanity, women need to change misperceptions and misunderstandings —even if it is unfair that *we* have to take the initiative.

- **Contribute and make a positive difference.** The culture *has* changed in the last 30 years. Authority in business will probably never be an equal 50/50 split of men and women. But we need to work towards the day when we stop expecting everyone to be the same, when we learn greater flexibility and tolerance in the work place, and in the world as well.

Author of **Marketing to Women**
and **PrimeTime Women**

MARTHA BARLETTA

Ms. Barletta is an internationally recognized consultant on successful marketing and selling to women. Her lively presentation style and practical suggestions make her a popular speaker. She has been featured in *The San Francisco Examiner, The London Free Press, Dagens Industri* (Sweden), *The Toronto Star, Brandweek, Strategy, Marketing, PROMO, Yahoo! Business Journal* and other publications. ■ Prior to launching The TrendSight Group, Ms. Barletta was VP, director, and creator of Frankly Female at Frankel, a leading brand marketing and promotion agency. She had spent several years managing the agency's packaged goods business unit for clients including Kodak, Nestle, Equal, Dial, and General Mills. ■ Before expanding into promotion,

Ms. Barletta spent ten years in the advertising business, culminating as VP/Account Director at Foote, Cone & Belding, Chicago, responsible for many award winning campaigns. ■ Ms. Barletta serves as the Marketing and Fundraising Chair for the National Women's History Museum, and chairs the Women's Marketing Council of the Business Women's Network, both in Washington DC. She lives and works near Chicago, IL. Visit www.trendsight.com.

Melissa Giovagnoli

Ms. Giovagnoli is one of the world's leading experts on the development of individual and community networks as a means of growing and accelerating brand loyalty inside and outside organizations. Her focus is on optimum career development and knowledge management. ■ For more than a decade, Ms. Giovagnoli's organization, Networlding, has provided exceptionally successful viral and relationship marketing programs for companies like AT&T, CNA, Motorola, and Disney. On the Advisory Board for the Women's Leadership Exchange, she also serves as an advisor to the University of Chicago's business school. She is a prolific writer and speaker with inexhaustible energy, planning foundations, events, and authoring many books. An urban pioneer, she lives and works in Chicago, IL. Visit www.networlding.com.

Strategically seek relationships with potential alliances, carefully find the right people to reflect and share in your purpose. Use caring and commonality to connect.

Build Value-Based Collaborations

by Melissa Giovagnoli

Believing that more can be accomplished by teaming up with others, strategically seek relationships with potential alliances. Develop skills that can grow:

- **Invite those you admire to collaborate.** Use caring and commonality to connect. When you have causes in common, the relationship becomes natural and inspiring. Give as you are also asking to get. If you promote others that inspire you, it builds a trust where they will then gladly help you.

- **Create events that link your community to sponsors.** Be creative and come up with benefits, marketing alliances, conferences, contests, publications, invitations, or educational opportunities.

- **Empower the women you know to help other women.** To support others can not only build their self-esteem but also your credibility. Confi-dence means to trust. There are many prosperous women who want to support good causes, but won't if not asked.

- **Donate a benefit** to an organization you believe in, or volunteer at a local association or school. Use an example of the results you achieve for promotions to those you know and for public relations to those you don't.

- **Practice flexibility.** If you find dead-ends or brick walls in response to your ideas, try a different approach. First, expand your idea to better serve by adding benefits. Next, seek additional alliances, patrons, or sponsors. Share interests with others. However, if you've approached the wrong person, or if the idea is still met with resistance, you may need to take your plans elsewhere.

There is always a way to achieve your concept if there is a market for it. Build alliances, partnerships, and mentorships by carefully finding the right people to reflect and share in your purpose. Think of it like making baklava: lay one sweet layer upon another.

Ms. Giovagnoli is author of and/or co-author of: *75 Cage Rattling Questions to Change the Way You Work: Shake-Em-Up Questions to Open Meetings, Ignite Discussion, and Spark Creativity; 50 Fabulous Places to Raise Your Family; Angels in the Workplace: Stories and Inspirations for Creating a New World of Work; Networlding: Building Relationships and Opportunities for Success; The Power of Two: How Companies of All Sizes Can Build Alliance Networks That Generate Business Opportunities;* and *Make Your Connections Count: The Six-Step System to Build Your Meganetwork*

Because each of us only has finite time and energy, apply resources where they can do the most good. This is the only fulfilling strategy. Look to grievances within your own experience to discover conviction.

Any efforts to spearhead change in a workplace have to be grounded in a solid understanding of the organization's mission; the agendas of those you work for; and the degree of maneuvering room you have (both officially and unofficially). All career strategy boils down to the interpersonal.

— Melissa Everett,
Making a Living While Making a Difference

We must make it known that we are ready to lead, that, in fact, we demand it, not only to fulfill the promise of democracy, but also to save it from a laundry list of ills. We have our minds, we have our communities, we have our votes, we have our wallets—we have our ability to influence the next generation. These are rich natural resources. Once we start mining them, leadership is inevitable.

— Marie C. Wilson, *Closing the Leadership Gap*

"Successful entrepreneurs are consummate networkers who know that relationship-building is the essential link to capital, employees, strategic alliance partners, and those who contribute to their future success. Circulate, get out, and get connected. Identify venue where prospective contacts gather—and go there. Alumni groups, trade organizations, industry councils—all are 'connecting' spots.

— Sharon Whiteley, Kathy Elliott, and Connie Duckworth, *The Old Girls' Network*

To achieve a results-only work environment:

• Stop doing any activity that is a waste of time.

• Employees have the freedom to work any way they want, as long as the work gets done.

• Nobody talks about how many hours they work.

• There are no work schedules.

• There is no judgment about how you spend your time.

— Cali Ressler and Jody Thompson,
Why Work Sucks and How to Fix It

New media multiples your relationships so that you can build your own community. Start by fostering a relationship based on two-way communication, in which the customer, not you, is at the heart of your communication. Your community sees your business as indispensable in meeting its needs and wants. Building an online community is the single most important thing you can do to grow your business.

— Lena Claxton and Alison Woo,
How to Say It: Marketing with New Media

AMBITION

Inner beliefs determine how we act, how others treat us, and how well we grow. If we connect through our values, we find shortcuts to profitable exchanges. The wise teach that behavior can only be as strong as the self-knowledge of our intrinsic characters. Ambition amplifies integrity: it exemplifies how well we match our nature to our circumstances, to our goals, and how well we coexist with others.

LEGACY LADIES

✳ **Don't compromise yourself. You are all you've got.**
— Janis Joplin

✳ **Blessed is he who has it in his power to do evil, yet does it not.**
— Marguerite of Navarre

✳ **When you make a world tolerable for yourself, you make a world tolerable for others.**
— Anaïs Nin

✳ **Integrity can be neither lost nor concealed nor faked nor quenched nor artificially come by nor outlived, nor, I believe, in the long run denied.**
— Eudora Welty

This mini-collection represents our roots— wisdom many may have grown up with. These idea-seeds encourage genetic progression: if we share what we know, then we can prepare for storms. Gardens need to be resilient. (See this collection grow online.)

Growing to Grow

by Lexi Reese

Growing to a million-dollar level is a process. These practices for such growth are demonstrated by those who will reach that mark and beyond:

- **Set a vision for growth.** Fill in this sentence: 'I want to be the pre-eminent ____.' You can't begin if you don't have a vision of where you want to be.

- **Develop a business plan.** If you don't have one, then write one!

- **Describe a business model that supports your vision.** This sounds obvious, but many entrepreneurs focus their efforts on having a perfect office, when their office isn't the thing that's going to grow their business! Instead, make sure you're having 15 client meetings a day (or getting a sales person to have those 15 client meetings a day).

- **Name three things that most hold you back.** Hone in on what you must improve. For example, if you are a web-based company and don't have the right technology, you're not going anywhere fast! If you're a service-based company, make sure that you have a robust profitable client base. Identify what your growth points are and focus on those.

- **Seek the right support.** What holds women back is a combination of money, mentoring, and marketing. Identify a source of help for each challenge. Shore up those tasks you may not be able to handle yourself.

- **Identify the next step to take in each challenge.** Invest in the technology or education that will help make your vision come alive.

- **Be selective about financing.** Don't take whatever capital comes your way. If you have short-term financing needs, take out a line of credit. If you need to make a longer-term capital investment, then take out a loan to pay back over time.

- **Seek and retain the best help.** You can never invest enough time in hiring the right people. Surround yourself with smart people who are better at certain tasks than you are—especially those tasks that you don't wake up in the morning loving to do. For example, if you are great at business development, you should be in front of clients and then outsource back-end processes. However, *never* relinquish control over core aspects of your business! *Manage* those aspects, even though you don't need to do the details yourself.

- **Develop a willingness to let go.** What it takes to start a business is not what it takes to grow one. What it takes to start is dogged self-reliance—an 'I'm going to do everything to get this business off the ground' attitude. What it takes to grow is delegating tasks to experts so you can work on your core business and not on the details. All small business owners have issues with delegation as they grow.

- **Recognize new areas of help.** There's a fatigue after having started up a business, having sustained the energies, resources, financing, and time it takes to grow. There's not much support after start-up but before reaching a million-dollars. So there's a big opportunity for new enterprises to support businesses that want to grow.

LEXI REESE

Ms. Reese helps deliver on American Express OPEN's commitment to serve the small business community by connecting women entrepreneurs with comprehensive business solutions. She oversees strategic marketing alliances with premium women's business associations, including the Women Presidents' Organization, the National Association of Women Business Owners, the Women's Leadership Exchange, and the Center for Women's Business Research. Together with these partner organizations, Ms. Reese sponsors networking and information exchange opportunities designed to help women-owned firms achieve their growth goals. ■ Ms. Reese has held a number of roles within American Express. In addition to her current position, she worked in the Corporate Services Division on strategic investments and acquisitions. ■ Prior to American Express, Ms. Reese held positions at Explo-rador Capital and ACCION International. She earned her MBA from Harvard Business School and is a Phi Beta Kappa graduate from the University of Virginia. She works in New York, NY. Visit www.makemineamillion.org.

As one woman business owner rises, **all** *women business owners rise.*

Nell Merlino

As co-founder and CEO of Count Me In for Women's Economic Independence, Ms. Merlino is also the founder and President of Strategy Communication Action, Ltd. in New York City, a firm specializing in the creation of public education campaigns that motivate action. She created and produced many dynamic and highly effective national and international business development efforts including the successful Take Our Daughters To Work Day, now an annual event in the United States and in dozens of countries worldwide.  After graduating from college, Ms. Merlino organized union health care workers, served two state governments, and contributed to several presidential campaigns. She played an active role in the strategic planning and management of the State University Medical School & Hospital in Brooklyn as chief of staff to the institution's president. ■ In 1989, Ms. Merlino started her own business. For her work on behalf of women, girls and families, she is recognized in many books and magazines, and newspapers, including the Woman of the Year Award by *New Woman* magazine and the Fulbright Award for Outstanding Achievement. ■ Ms. Merlino lives in New York, NY with her husband. Visit her at www.countmein.org. Author of **Stepping Out of Line**

Master a Million Dollar Mindset

by Nell Merlino

Success is knowing which rules you can break and which rules you must play by. Successful women entrepreneurs courageously overcome barriers that are both systemic and personal—they are so determined to grow their businesses that they develop fighting techniques to overcome resistance:

- **Be aggressive to achieve.** If you wait for someone to call to see how you're doing, you're never going to get there. The women who are willing on a daily basis to ask for help will. Those that are 'too busy' to seek assistance are trying to do everything themselves! They won't make their goals because they aren't open to help.

- **Accept mistakes.** Every entrepreneur is going to make them—and you're going to make them with *your* money! It often seems you might as well put the funds on the floor and set a match to them! Not the most effective use of resources! But it might have been! And you can't be successful all the time! But you can to do it if you learn and move on!

- **Articulate your strategy.** Figure out how to navigate through the challenges. Or ignore them and say, 'I'll just keep playing to my strengths. I'm good at X, so it will carry me along.' But at some point, you must assemble all the necessary pieces to progress.

- **Shift your source of pride.** Most awardees of the Make Mine a Million Program initially say: 'I've done this all myself and I haven't borrowed any money.' So they reveal why they're stuck. You really can't go much further if you are by yourself: there's only so many hours in the day, so much brain power, etc. If you haven't borrowed any money, you can't leverage or grow.

- **Know what you want.** Women finally have permission to think of themselves as million-dollar business owners. This is a permission to go crazy and tell yourself and others what you want to create. Where do you want to end up? Obviously you have to deal with the reality of business now, but what do you see? You can't make it if you can't see it! What would the headline be? Then plan backwards from there.

- **Delegate.** Women believe that to prove themselves, they have to do everything because so often in home situations, if they don't do it, it doesn't happen. Often we take at-home behavior and apply it to work—like multitasking. If you want to grow, you can't multitask to the million dollar level! Recognize and use the resources around you!

- **Don't wait.** For centuries, women have been waiting—for people to call, to choose them as mates, etc. But business requires flipping *out* of that mentality! So many women have a great product or service and are literally waiting for it to be recognized. But it is you who has to generate the interest!

- **Incorporate relationships.** Get others invested in your success: customers, employees, family, and network. Convince them that *your* success is *their* success.

- **Create measurements.** Workers want leaders who focus and results which are tangible. They are encouraged by visible milestones.

- **Look beyond money.** Financing is always an issue—like losing that last ten pounds. But if you do these other things, the money will come.

"

You must have the courage to take risks, stir up controversy, be talked about behind your back, and talked back to by the opposition. *And* until a woman can change her un-evil ways, be tough, bear balls, face controversy, and *stop* caring what people think, then others—both men and women others—will forever have an edge over her.

— Karen Salmansohn,
How to Succeed In Business Without a Penis

"

"

When you see the higher service in your work, you will bring a spiritual dimension, understanding, appreciation, and code of ethics to what you do at work *every single day*.

— Susan and Larry Terkel, *Small Change*

Act like an entrepreneur. Even if you are working within an organization, work hard to run it as efficiently as if you owned it.

— Sharon K. Young as quoted by Dr. Margot B. Weinstein, *7 Steps to Find Your Perfect Career*

"

There are times when it is helpful to set goals, and other times when it is best to let go for a while and just see where life takes you. Goals help us gain clarity, inspiration, and focus. However, they can also work against us if we hold onto them too tightly, or try *too* hard to make them happen. Let the higher creative power handle the details and let your inner guidance show you the way.

— Shakti Gawain, *Creating True Prosperity*

The art of life is not controlling what happens to us, but *using* what happens to us.

— Gloria Steinem, *Revolution from Within*

All broken relationships can be traced back to broken agreements. If you want self-respect, if you want to stand out in the business community, if you want great relationships, and if you want to be trusted, keep your word.

— Fran Hewitt, *The Power of Focus for Women*

"

What you believe based upon the prevailing psychological theory can either prevent or promote change. Ideas regarding causes create a reality for you. Exploring and changing the questions you ask yourself and the theories you create in response to your experiences can change your life in a surprisingly powerful way. The thinking solution helps you ask the right questions.

— Pat Hudson, *The Solution Oriented Woman*

"

PURPOSE

The only way to have harmony between meaning and money is through purpose. When we feel that our direction matters, we discover deep conviction to sustain any activity despite tests and challenges. Once found, purpose plants the seeds and nurtures the garden into a momentum of growth. Wise women cross-pollinate purposes throughout their various activities and life phases, strengthening resiliency.

LEGACY LADIES

✳ **An aim in life is the only fortune worth finding.**
— JACQUELINE KENNEDY ONASSIS

✳ **I've never sought success in order to get fame and money; it's the talent and the passion that count.**
— INGRID BERGMAN

✳ **That is happiness: to be dissolved into something complete and great.**
— WILLA SIBERT CATHER

✳ **If God lets me live, I shall attain more than Mummy ever has done, I shall not remain insignificant, I shall work in the world and for mankind!**
— ANNE FRANK

This mini-collection represents our roots—wisdom many may have grown up with. These idea-seeds encourage genetic progression: if we share what we know, then we can prepare for storms. Gardens need to be resilient. (See this collection grow online.)

The Destiny Path

by Susan Davis

It is difficult to juggle family and business in this competitive fear-based 'career' system. Instead of struggling, go to a deeper level. Realize that we each have a Destiny Path far more significant than our career path. We are *not* in competition because no one else has our purpose. If we follow our Destiny Path versus our Career Path, we will find joy, for joy comes from taking risks around our values. The journey entails several practice components if we seek it within our work:

- **Show business generosity.** If we help others, we will attract generous people who will help lessen both our risks and our stresses.

- **Manifest our values.** To declare and pursue spiritual values is a good way to conduct business because companies have souls the way that people do. Examples of good practices are:

  - A deal is a good deal when it is good for all concerned.
  - Generosity comes back ten-fold … to the bottom line.
  - Truth is always the best policy.
  - A call of complaint is welcome because it lets us improve.

- **Provide high-tech with high-touch.** E-mail is a socially responsible way to communicate because we are not killing trees and it provides geographic flexibility. Use the technology, but balance it with strategic phone calls to discuss emotional issues and to keep our hearts connected with our business associates.

- **Maintain a socially responsible company.** Instead of 'shareholder capitalism' (which addresses the interests of only investors), practice 'stakeholder capitalism' (which addresses the varied interests of customers, employees, investors, suppliers, and community). Socially-responsible companies have been shown to financially outperform others. (See CapitalMissions.com, 'Triple Bottom Line Simulation')

- **Compensate for an educational system that is too analytical.** We are educated that we must train our minds and discount our emotions as 'subjective.' But our emotions serve our intuition, which is our direct connection with our soul. Learn to trust intuition in making business decisions within the context of our Destiny Path.

- **Hear lessons in events.** September 11, 2001, was a wake up call for many who follow a Career Path. It showed that only taking risks around our values to find our Destiny Paths was what would bring satisfaction. This single event dramatically fueled the socially responsible business revolution. It has given us the courage to follow our hearts and create unique ways to serve others.

The explosive growth of the socially-responsible business sector shows us how many millions of people are now committed to finding joy by insisting on it in our work—thus creating our paths....
Our Destiny Paths.

Take risks around values. Be true and responsible to intuition. This is how we find a Destiny Path, which will give us the deepest joy.

SUSAN DAVIS

Ms. Davis left a division administrator position for Harris Bank's Personal Trust Group after nine years to start Capital Missions Company (CMC), a social venture consulting firm. Her company creates networks of investors who expect market returns plus social and environmental dividends. Ms. Davis forms these networks by using a proprietary nine-step program. CMC's first network was the Investors' Circle supplying venture capital to socially responsible companies. ■ Over the last 25 years, Ms. Davis has helped to start five major social ventures and launched one of the country's first "cause-related marketing programs." Ms. Davis is pivotal in launching national organizational networks for: top women business owners (Committee of 200), for very wealthy families (Harris Bank Family Office Management Conference), and for social venture entrepreneurs (Social Venture Network). ■ Ms. Davis received a Bachelor of Arts Cum Laude in Russian from Brown University and did graduate work in anthropology at the Harvard Graduate School of Education. She lives and works in an eco-village in Elkhorn, WI. Visit www.capitalmissions.com.

LESLIE GROSSMAN

Ms. Grossman is a 'serial entrepreneur.' Since the age of 23, she has launched or run five companies—all in marketing, public relations, and event management—and all geared to reaching women. Perhaps best known for her six-year campaign to rejuvenate platinum jewelry, Ms. Grossman now lives her passion—to create more women leaders. A past president of several business associations, including the National Association of Women Business Owners (NAWBO), New York Women's Association, Women's Leadership Forum, SBA National Advisory Council, and Fashion Group International, Ms. Grossman integrates her passion with her expertise. She has served on many advisory boards, including the Center for Women's Business Research. As president of B2Women, she develops win-win marketing programs for corporations and women business leaders. As co-founder of Women's Leadership Exchange, she supports women leading companies through a multi-channel communications and conference program. ■ A frequent speaker, Ms. Grossman has traveled internationally and is interviewed frequently on women's business issues. She has been honored with many awards including the NAWBO National Leadership Award. She lives and works in New York, NY.

Visit www.womensleadershipexchange.com.

Purpose as a Discovery

by Leslie Grossman

Purpose means following your passions to reach your goals. The higher the goals you set, the closer you get to them. If your goals are realistic, then you've set your sites too short! Women are limited by what they don't know, even about their own purposes and potentials. It is when these qualities come together that women can find the greatest fulfillment and meaning in their work. To ensure that you are on the path of your best efforts:

- **Do personal growth work.** Take the time to ask yourself what you feel most passionate about. Explore workshops or seminars that may help.

- **Pursue the Magical Question.** By asking a probing and insightful question, you set the energy for a new direction to move. This usually comes at a time of business change—or when you need to rekindle your passions. There is great power in the visionary question! In fact, one question can change your whole direction into the opportunity of your dreams! Passion eases dramatic shifts and changes.

- *Use* **crisis to advantage.** Change makes you ask the hard questions! You have to inquire: 'why is this happening?' There is always something powerful to learn.

- **See signs.** Watch for the elements of how things come together. There are signals that lead you forward. It is most exciting when all of your experiences start coming together! And it is when opportunities, connections, and skills fall together that you know you are on the right track.

- **Be responsive.** Get the market need and your passion to form a purpose when combined. Use your experience in a bigger way. Identify what you can address *with* your passion.

- **Make mistakes.** Many women find themselves facing challenges for which they really are not prepared. But even mistakes can benefit you! You may even learn the most from them.

- **Accept no excuses.** Determine your purpose and then find solutions to obstacles as you go. Don't let limitations stop you!

Living your passion can be much bigger than your original plans. Learn to focus on what matters most and you will find that your sense of purpose will take you there.

Author of *Sellsation!*

Get the market need and your passion to come together and form a purpose. Use your experience in a bigger way.

Make sure you have at least one task or appointment each day that moves you toward a bigger goal, or else the scenery will never change.

— Liz Davenport, *Order from Chaos: a Six-Step Plan for Organizing Yourself, Your Office, and Your Life*

Set up a business plan for your life. A plan forces you to think about what you truly want. Write a personal plan based on the segments of a traditional one.

— Aliza Sherman, *Power Tools for Women in Business*

" There are a lot of things that are worth more if you save them for later, but your happiness isn't one of them. Plan for the future all you want, but don't make the mistake of putting your life on hold until it gets there. The best times of women's lives are when they can put pressure aside and just enjoy doing one thing for a moment.

— Lisa Earle McLeod, *Forget Perfect* "

No longer do what's insignificant or unimportant in the scheme of corporate goals. Instead, work on what is important and get that perfect. Then delegate the rest with the necessary follow-up to ensure your team gets it right. Only by doing or creating significant work can women break the mold of being nurturers who can always be counted on for the grunt work.

— Janice Reals Ellig and William J. Morin,
What Every Successful Woman Knows

"Attract your customer's attention. Get them involved with a survey, a contest, or a publicity stunt. When they feel they have invested part of themselves in your business, they will want to share that alliance with others. Use every resource at your disposal to get people talking. Whether it is a wacky e-mail message or a special incentive included on an invoice, make even mundane communication something to talk about.

— Lynn Thorne,
Word-of-Mouth Advertising Online and Off

The first half of our life is spent chasing success; the second half is chasing significance.

— Cathie Black, *Basic Black*

Highly change-resilient people view service as their true mission and hold material wealth as secondary. They have a strong sense of belonging and understand the value of nurturing relationships. In serving others from caring and connectedness, many of their own deepest needs can also be fulfilled.

— Michelle and Joel Levey, *Living in Balance*

FOCUS

When we are dedicated to growing a business, what we focus on determines our fate. To control attention, prepare the field of business with knowledge gained from observation. Learn from the past, experience the present completely, and imagine the future. Read the sky for coming weather, but don't forget to weed out distractions that choke or dilute current efforts. Focus is our greatest choice and greatest power.

LEGACY LADIES

✳ **The less said the better.**
— JANE AUSTEN

✳ **Time is a very precious gift of God; so precious that it's only given to us moment by moment.**
— AMELIA BARR

✳ **To tend, unfairingly, unflinchingly, towards a goal, is the secret of success.**
— ANNA PAVLOVA

✳ **I've learned ruthless concentration. I can write under any circumstances . . . street noises, loud talk, music, you name it.**
— SYLVIA PORTER

This mini-collection represents our roots— wisdom many may have grown up with. These idea-seeds encourage genetic progression: if we share what we know, then we can prepare for storms. Gardens need to be resilient. (See this collection grow online.)

Healing Attention

by Roxanna Trinka

Our lives become what we focus on, pay attention to, or surround ourselves with. Regardless of circumstances, *you* are responsible for what your life looks like. Being diagnosed with cancer can be an opportunity to test this theory. Conscious decisions about who and what will play a role in the cure takes precedence and teaches many lessons. When faced with any adversity it's important to:

- **Focus on what you want the outcome to be**—then miracles are invited. Set the atmosphere for what you want to happen.

- **Recognize the needs of others to avoid feeling sorry for yourself.** There are those with greater challenge and more hardship than you. What a *wonderful* revelation: 'It's not about me! It's about everyone else!'

- **'What you resist persists!'** Don't *fight* what happens. Accept that the cancer (or death, divorce, or bankruptcy, etc.) happened and realize you have to 'drive your own bus.' Deal with the treatments or solutions as well as do everything in your power to prevent the illness (or the problem) from recurring.

- **Surround yourself with people committed to your outcome.** Increase your endurance with the *right* help. What you focus on, the friends you choose, and the professionals providing your treatment make all the difference, so choose well!

- **Live fully *right now*!** Do *more* than you think you can. Volunteer and donate *more* than you have been. You'll be amazed at the results! Joy and fulfillment can be found, regardless of diagnosis, supposed prognosis, or negative predictions.

- **Find the joy in your work.** If you can't find any, you probably are in the wrong profession. What do you have to lose if you stay unhappy? What do you have to gain if you do what you love? Look at the big picture. Did your job *contribute* to your difficulties? Can employees and customers be enrolled in your decision to thrive? The result *can* be that they thrive too!

- **Choose your attitude like you choose your clothes in the morning.** Be responsible, for attitude is contagious! Laughter and optimism lessen the side effects of remedies. A positive attitude causes others to want to be around you, no matter how dire your situation.

- **Just say 'no' to the Pity Party.** Don't go there: the company's lousy and the hangover's worse!

These are not suggestions just for those who are ill or failing. Don't wait to *become* ill to learn the value of health! Difficulties provide lessons that can carry over into wellness. Pay attention to discover the meaning. Give joy to every experience and your reward will be further joy.

Everything that happens to you enriches you, teaches you, and gives you the ability to move forward, even when that movement is painful.

ROXANNA TRINKA

Ms. Trinka is the President/CEO of Baseline Engineering
& Land Surveying, Inc. She is also a Trustee member of
the Boca Raton Chamber of Commerce and the facilitator
for the chamber's Business Interest Group 'Public Policy &
Governmental Affairs' meetings. She has served on the City
of Boca Raton Zoning Board of Adjustment and ran for City
Council. Appointed to the Florida Atlantic Research and
Development Authority, Ms. Trinka established an on-campus
Research Park. Named Rotarian of the Year by the Boca Raton
Sunset Rotary Club, she is the secretary and serves as the Area
Foundation Team Leader and Area Polio Eradication Chair.

A recent breast cancer survivor, Ms. Trinka has launched
a Web site called YOUCANTHRIVE.COM designed to
be a source of empowerment, encouragement,
inspiration and support for those experiencing
any kind of hardship and to assist their family
members and friends. Ms. Trinka is also a
Board Member and Secretary for the Boca
Raton Police Athletic League, a Board Member
and mentor to The Haven (a therapeutic
residence for abused, neglected, or abandoned
boys), a Board Member for Children, Hope
& Horses, and she volunteers at Hospice by
the Sea Care Center. Ms Trinka works in
Boca Raton, FL. Visit www.baseline-eng.com.

JACKIE HUBA

Ms. Huba researches the effects of word of mouth on customer loyalty. As the co-author of two books, *The New York Times* called *Creating Customer Evangelists* 'the new mantra for entrepreneurial success.' This book has grown into a worldwide phenomenon and has been translated into six languages. As an example of what word of mouth can trigger, prior to the book's release, Google returned only two mentions of the term 'customer evangelists.' Today, the search engine finds hundreds of thousands of citations! ■ As a business advisor, Huba has worked with Microsoft, Ulta, Discovery Education, Yahoo, and Verio as well as thousands of small and medium businesses. Prior, she led B-2-B marketing efforts for twelve years at IBM in its software division. She is a board member of the Word of Mouth Marketing Association and a graduate of Penn State University. ■ Her work in researching passionate customer loyalty has been profiled by the *Wall Street Journal*, *The New York Times*, *Fortune*, *Businessweek*, *U.S. News & World Report*, *The Financial Times*, *Fast Company* and several thousand blogs. She lives and works in Austin, TX. Visit www.customevangelists.com.

Help Your Prospects Find You

by Jackie Huba

New tools expand traditional marketing: they extend your reach and possibilities. From traveling the country and speaking to thousands of professionals, here is the best advice to generate professional visibility:

- **Promote by making offers.** Build in-bound referrals. If you depend on out-bound marketing, you have to follow up, and the conversion rate is much lower than if you get really great in-bound referrals who are ready to do business. Approach your best industry hubs, but not in a way that is 'salesy.' Don't send out a direct mail with the approach: 'we're great; can we work with you?' Instead, think of opportunities for prospects to be part of something. This allows those that are interested to respond—because the last thing you want to do is chase leads who aren't interested! Instead, just follow up with those who say 'yes, I want what you are selling.' Do everything you can to attract *qualified* prospects.

- **Become an 'in'-person.** Network where your audience is. The number one thing you can do for your business (no matter what kind of business) is speak. If you can tell a story about what you do, you share your knowledge. Then people say 'Oh, she knows about what I'm trying to do—I should do business with her.' Go places you wouldn't ordinarily think of, like joining a networking group or marketing association. The in-person attracts prospects.

- **Build your web site.** Development may be a little slow at first. But in the long term, you will spend less on marketing because people will find you or refer business to you. Over 80% of prospects check up on professionals online before they do business with them. So if you have nothing online for visitors, they might just go to the next search result!

- **Set online goals.** Know how much participation you want and then come up with tactics to attract that level. Some approaches will work; some won't work, so try many.

- **Create a blog.** Even if you are in a corporation, build your personal brand because you never know what will happen. By having a blog, people searching will find you.

- **Monitor your Google position.** When people type in your name or search terms related to you, appear high so that you can be found.

- **Give a personal touch to current customers.** So many people focus on getting *new* customers. But this is expensive and time-consuming. It is better to inspire current customers to refer business to you. Give them small things—a thank you note, flowers, a book, or treat them to an event. Most importantly, ask them: 'would you refer us?' These personal touches are the most important part of your marketing.

- **Ask your network for help.** Start a breakfast for those who want to talk about issues. The great thing about women business owners is their sense of community. So many are willing to help other women!

- **Utilize virtual assistants.** We don't have any employees—all helpers are outside. They schedule our events, arrange travel, work with contact companies, and accounts receivable. By the hour, we can afford people who are specialists. Take advantage of new expertise!

Dancing on Your Toes

by Hedy Ratner

Preference keeps many women-owned businesses small—especially for those with only a part-time commitment. Entrepreneurial women need to have the time, passion, commitment, and support to build a business. Also, the credibility of women's business ownership and the depth of knowledge, experience, and success (or potential for success) are not yet acknowledged in the larger community. Though women are now almost half of all businesses in the U.S., the decision-makers in power haven't realized or accepted this fact. The most common challenges that face women affect each not as individuals, but as a whole. Here are the most important business-building considerations:

- **Create credibility and opportunities.** The economic case to do business with women owners is clear. We're the major consumers, the major buyers, even becoming the major decision-makers. As the demographics change, we also comprise the largest number of employees. The financial community is just beginning to be aware of these facts.

- **Identify business priorities.** The choice of business model keeps many women-owned companies small. Perhaps the owner has not found a niche that can grow or may be *thinking* too small. But then there's thinking too big by not being realistic about the possibilities. Men don't seem to have the same emotional attachment to their businesses as women do. Men *believe* they are going to achieve and may try two or three or four businesses before they are successful. Women tend to prepare more than men going into business—because we don't want to take the risk of being wrong. Yet often we make a limiting decision *despite* the knowledge that we have! We say 'This is what I *want* to do, so this is what I'm *going* to do!' But this may not be the wisest thing to do! Get as much help as possible so we're not overwhelmed. Or maybe we're still overwhelmed, but at least we've got our priorities straight.

- **Develop profitability.** There are many women who have no idea if their businesses can make money! We've seen some in business for years that don't know if they've made money or not; they just keep going. They could be losing or coming out even. Gain education, resources, and the expertise needed to make the right decisions. With knowledge, we become more confident. Or we'll learn that our concept doesn't work. And that's more important than anything!

- **Encourage access to capital.** Many women who have great ideas and passion are economically disadvantaged. When a bank, invest-ment, or venture capital firm have women officers at high levels, women borrowers find the access to capital easier. But the more we can finance on our own, the more opportunities open to accelerate later!

- **Seek political action.** Many businesswomen are so single-minded and directed, they have no idea what is going on politically and don't realize it has any impact on business! But we must have awareness because it influences operations policies. Read the newspaper, trade magazines, and be on top of issues—we don't have time *not* to!

- **Nurture support system.** Families are often unsupportive of a woman-owned business because it takes time and energy away from them. Develop a support system that isn't family: include friends, organizations, or resources that can best help. We can't do it alone!

HEDY RATNER

As the founder and co-president of the Women's Business Development Center, the largest, oldest, and most comprehensive women's business assistance center in the U.S., Ms. Ratner helps develop women's business programs nationally. The Center provides counseling, training, financial, certification, and procurement assistance for emerging and established women business owners. ■ Prior, Ms. Ratner served as the President of the Chicago Institute for Economic Development, the Executive Director of the Chicago Film and Video Studio Foundation, and headed her own public relations firm. Her early experience as a teacher/librarian led to positions in the Superintendent's Office of Cook County Schools and the U.S. Office of Education. ■ In addition to being appointed by President Clinton to the National Women's Business Council, she has been appointed by a series of Illinois governors to serve on many counsels and commissions. ■ She has also served on task forces for minority and women's business enterprise issues for the city and state, is a board member of the Chicagoland Chamber of Commerce and The Chicago Convention and Tourism Bureau. Her honors include the Lifetime Achievement Award from Rainbow PUSH, the Compass Award from the Women's Leadership Exchange, the SBA Women's Business Advocate of the Year, among others. ■ With a Masters degree from DePaul University and the University of Chicago, she lives and works in Chicago, IL. Visit www.wbdc.org.

> In most industries, you win people over by entertaining them. You must serve information up in such a way that it can't be ignored.

— Linda Kaplan Thaler and Robin Koval,
Bang! Getting Your Message Heard in a Noisy World

> The direction that women consumers take—like wanting to know more about a brand than its price and positioning—is the way all consumers are headed. Be awake, attuned to details, relationship-oriented, and process-aware.

— Faith Popcorn, *EVEolution*

"

Keep your eye on your *own* goal, rather than play to the screams of the crowd. You might compete, for instance, to be the most creative or innovative. You might compete to be a real leader of great wisdom and insight. You might compete to make the most intelligent contributions. These would be competitions worthy of your deepest ambition.

— Linda Austin, M.D., *What's Holding You Back?*

"

"When you grow your business to the next level, you'll find you don't have to burn the midnight oil every night. You'll have a social life again. You don't have to be the chief cook and bottle washer. You can step back from the day-to-day management activities. You'll come closer to achieving the flexibility you may have been looking for when you started your business in the first place, because you have grown out of the survival mode.

— Susan Wilson Solovic,
The Girl's Guide to Building a Million-Dollar Business"

Conflict is unavoidable. It stems from the vast differences in the way people get things done. By surrounding yourself with your conative clones you can artificially remove conflict, but you'll replace it with inertia. The issue with conflict is not to lessen it but to manage it. Give others the same freedom to be themselves that you yourself need.

— Kathy Kolbe, *The Conative Connection*

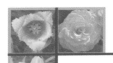

PERSPECTIVE

Immersed in our work, businesses, families, and responsibilities, we often get lost in our own worlds. Wisdom inspires experiences to deepen understanding and meaning. The greatest perspectives are the dearest earned. As the tree grows, it forms rings and throws branches to the sky as it digs its roots deeper into the earth's foundation. A perspective of one tree can lead us to the forest and increase our chances to flourish.

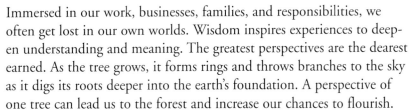

LEGACY LADIES

✳ **Miracles surround us at every turn if we but sharpen our perceptions of them.**
— WILLA CATHER

✳ **They sicken of calm, who know the storm.**
— DOROTHY PARKER

✳ **We don't see people as they are, we see them as we are.**
— ANAÏS NIN

✳ **If we could sell our experiences for what they cost us, we'd all be millionaires.**
— ABIGAIL VAN BUREN

This mini-collection represents our roots— wisdom many may have grown up with. These idea-seeds encourage genetic progression: if we share what we know, then we can prepare for storms. Gardens need to be resilient. (See this collection grow online.)

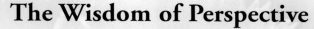

The Wisdom of Perspective

by Alexandra Stoddard

Happiness is a choice—the wisest we can make. It is an inner commitment to ourselves. Happiness lies in the passions we pursue and the pressures we decline:

- **Happiness cultivates a clear point-of-view.** We must train our mind to literally 'see through' what is negative. When we establish an attitude that is life-affirming, full of hope, faith and optimism, our energy is used constructively. We improve our decision-making and overall well-being when guided by values of truth, goodness, and beauty.

- **Practice continual mindfulness.** This is the capacity to be fully present in each moment. It leads to self-awareness and we grow into the light of our higher consciousness. We think *through* this luminescent prism to shape our habits, character, and conscience—living with greater depth and meaning.

- **Happiness is the energy force to nurture mental health which then affects physical health.** Write ten words that are defining and then be true to these concepts in all decisions and directions. Mine are:

love, sunlight, gardens, beaches, children, food, family, color, ribbons, and home. Each of us has our unique set of images to guide us.

- **Use intuition to set priorities.** Aristotle asked, 'What is the good life?' He believed we should trust and be guided by intuition. One of my challenges is carving out enough time to think and write. What works best for me is to get up early, get right to work, and put in two extra hours seven days a week.

- **Control attitude.** It would be hard to have wisdom without the balance of perspective. When we love ourselves, when we love life, when we love others, we will be happy, and when we achieve this high consciousness we will be resources to others. From the perspective of love, all good is possible in our short earthly lives. Be a cultivator of good, of perspective, and of love.

Author of ***Living a Beautiful Life***, ***Daring to Be Yourself***, ***The Art of the Possible***, ***Gracious Living in a New World***, ***Choosing Happiness***, and ***Time Alive: Celebrate Your Life Everyday***, among many others.

ALEXANDRA STODDARD

As an interior designer and acclaimed philosopher of contemporary living, Ms. Stoddard has shared her wisdom for more than 30 years. Her unique insights inspire a large and growing international following. In more than 20 books, she explains how to find and sustain happiness in everyday life. This original approach has resulted in appearances with *Oprah*, Barbara Walters and Katie Couric on the *Today Show*, appearances on the *Christopher Lowell Show*, *Home Matters*, and as a hostess of the Home & Garden television series *Homes Across America*. She is profiled in major magazines and newspapers worldwide. Ms. Stoddard's writing and talks contain a positive personal philosophy laced with grace, wit, and ritualizing every day—elevating interior design to the art of living beautifully moment to moment. ■ In 1963 Ms. Stoddard worked for the doyen of American Interior Design, Eleanor McMillen Brown, becoming her special assistant and close friend. After her mentor retired, Ms. Stoddard started her own international design firm, Alexandra Stoddard Incorporated. Ms. Stoddard is the founder and President of Design & Art Society, Ltd., and a Doyen of the American Society of the Order of St. John, designated by Queen Elizabeth II. ■ She lives in Carnegie Hill, Manhattan, New York City and Stonington Village, CN. Visit www.AlexandraStoddard.com.

CRISTINA TABORA

Ms. Tabora is the president and CEO of a boutique communications firm in New York, and is the managing partner of the Business Partnering Strategies firm in Manila. Her clients have included U.S.-based international travel and tourism companies such as Sandals Hotels & Resorts, Hyatt International Hotels, the Coastal Hotel Group, Military Historical Tours, and the Philippines Department of Tourism. Current developments in China and the Middle East include tourism, retail, cosmetics, brand franchise, and real estate construction projects. ■ Ms. Tabora also serves as a Trustee of the Ma-Yi Theatre Group, as Trustee and Executive Secretary of the Philippine Jesuit Foundation, and is a mentor for the Mentoring Program of the New York City Partnerships. ■ Prior to pursuing these endeavors, for nineteen years she was the Corporate Director of Communications for the Hyatt International Hotels Corporation. A graduate of Maryknoll College in the Philippines, she updated her core studies at Northwestern University.

■ Born in Manila on Christmas Eve explains a lot about her personality and global perspective. Having grown up in San Francisco and Manila, Ms. Tabora "fell in love with the English language as both pretty and as a powerful communication medium." She lives and works in New York, NY, and is the proud mother of two grown children. Visit www.taboracommunications.com.

International Perceptions

by Cristina Tabora

Glass ceilings and macho matrixes still exist, but women are being smarter and better humored about how to work around them. Why waste the time or energy to break them down? It's just another challenge to juggle. And no one—supervisor, peer, or subordinate—questions success! Working as a thriving international businesswoman does not involve sexist secrets but lessons to apply to *every* demographic:

- **Respect the culture, history, and traditions of the country you are engaging.** Never impose your native SOPs, but be willing to teach if asked. Say 'please' and 'thank you' always; say 'yes' more than 'no,' and give credit whenever and to whomever it is due. Try to master a few polite local language phrases, appreciate the local art, and eat the local food. Be aware to grow your understanding.

- **Do not be afraid to ask a question** when navigating through communication difficulties. People are very generous with sharing answers, but only with those who are not manipulative, embarrassed, or plain disinterested. There is such arrogance to glibness without knowledge! The flip side is the irresistible charm of self-effacing candor.

- **Utilize a corporate advantage.** Working for any multi-national company structure provides an invaluable umbrella of safety and reference. With a local office, you can fast-track into the culture, the social civilities, the current hot fashions, important people, watering holes… You also learn what political or issue buttons not to push unless you deliberately want to declare a position.

- **Do homework.** Without the help of an extended family that is the local office, be smart about researching as much as you can before arriving there. No excuse these days: anyone can Google!

- **Utilize entrepreneurial advantages.** Confidence and curiosity are in every entrepreneur's bag of tricks. The strategic mindset you develop is the most important advantage. Listen to the said *and* the unsaid! If you can't embrace a challenge or sense an opportunistic moment, you're better off working for someone who does. And if you can, always surround yourself with smart young people who make you smarter and keep you relevant.

- **Adapt to changed perceptions.** In the past, when walking the corridors of hotels, you could recognize the muffled sound of CNN on TVs behind many closed doors. It's no longer true that when America sneezes, the rest of the world catches a cold. The political axis of the world has changed, and may again. The Middle East and China are new lightning rods. Earth Day is not just the concern of Hug-A-Tree types. Wi-fi connectivity is no longer the priority of geeks. There are many new global news networks, including a growing grab of audiences by online reporting. And who'd have anticipated the power of the blog? If you want to be relevant as an internationalist, you better be on top of what's happening everywhere, using the type of medium with which you feel most comfortable.

This is a world ready for women of any age who are educated enough to know they can always learn more, and are enthusiastic to do so.

"The bottom line is that for all our obsession with money—getting it, spending it, saving it, investing it—having it has next to no effect on our happiness. True wealth isn't measured in assets or cash flow but in how abundant we feel. People who see possibilities in even the starkest reality can find happiness just about anywhere.

— Joan Duncan Oliver,
Happiness: How to Find It and Keep It

The purpose of emotions, regardless of what they are, is to help us feel and participate fully in our own lives. To become aware of our inner guidance system, we must learn to trust our emotions. If we don't heed the message the first time, we get hit with a bigger hammer the next time.

— Christiane Northrup, M.D.,
Women's Bodies, Women's Wisdom

The hardest thing to realize is that I can't fix it all and then begin to share that fixing it isn't the point at all. The point is being in the river and enjoying all the twists and turns, the rough parts and the calm. Sometimes destruction is a necessary part of the creative cycle. And challenges come to complete us.

— Pat B. Allen, *Art is a Way of Knowing*

Only when we recognize our commonalities rather than focus on what we perceive as differences do we join the human race.

— Jean Smith, *NOW! The Art of Being Truly Present*

Discover gratitude in the darkness, joy in the sadness, and life in the ruins, for the fit of a new perspective.

— Carol L. McClelland, Ph.D.,
The Seasons of Change

Ten Keys to Success:

1. Curiosity—be eager to learn.
2. Decisiveness—arrive at a conclusion.
3. Perseverance—desire results.
4. Empathy—understand someone else's situation.
5. Flexibility—be capable of change.
6. Follow-through—take the next step.
7. Humor—enjoy the world.
8. Intelligence—think smartly.
9. Optimism—expect the best outcome.
10. Respect—treat others in a considerate and courteous manner.

— Julie Johnson,
I Don't Know What I Want, But I Know It's Not This

> Now that we're grown-ups—out in the world with families to manage, businesses to run, competitors to vanquish, and battles to win—playing it small isn't safe; it's a threat to our happiness, our sense of fulfillment, our very purpose for being here.

— Deborah Rosado Shaw, *Dream Big!*

> Make sure all team members are clear on the S.M.E.A.C.: Situation, Mission, Execution strategy, Administrative needs, and Communication pipeline—for every project.

— Frances Cole Jones, *How to WOW*

It isn't enough to create a collaborative work environment. The leader must also exhibit the ability to make quick (and often controversial) decisions. The unpopular decisions are certainly among the toughest. You can seek consensus, but you must be able to stand alone when your principles mandate it. Solitude is an unavoidable condition of leadership.

— Candy Deemer and Nancy Fredericks,
Dancing on the Glass Ceiling

INDEX

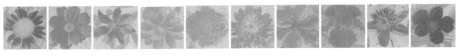

✳ Life is like a game of tennis. You've got to think ahead. You've got to be aggressive, because if you don't move ahead, you slip behind. Nobody stands still—in a career, in life. So get behind it and *shove*—that's the way to get it out of the mud—lean forward.
— KATHARINE HEPBURN

✳ Woman must not accept; she must challenge. She must not be awed by that which has been built up around her; she must reverence that woman in her which struggles for expression.
— MARGARET SANGER

Wisdom of Women

by Liane Sebastian

Winning women make femininity an advantage. As one of the few societies in history where female professionals are approaching an equal status with male professionals, we have the freedom and ability to form our careers the way that we choose. *How* we choose will influence not only the growth of possibilities for young women to come but for all women internationally!

Working with the contributors profiled in this book reveals a commonality of traits, experiences, opinions, and advice. All seem to agree, as if they were sitting down together, that learned skills combined with experience enhance potential efforts. Many agree that for any woman to be wise and to become a leader she must:

- **Do the work needed to know herself.** To resist the common plague of perfectionism, we have to prioritize. By knowing our values first, we can then connect meaningfully with others' values.

- **See advantages in femininity.** When we try to be like men, we don't do as well. We need to *enhance* our differences and make them work for us. We try not to duplicate solutions that work for men unless we can adapt them to especially use our strengths. Through observation, we can become more sensitive to others' working styles, *enhancing* our ability to adapt.

- **Use resources** through strategically developing beneficial contacts, skills, and research. We can masterfully benefit from our networks, finding that the effort we invest into them is matched by the benefits we receive. Competitors can transform into partnerships.

- **Ask for help** to free us from attempting more tasks than we can handle. We can't attain anything meaningful unless we let go of activities that have little meaning. If we differentiate our unique contributions from work that someone else can do better, helpers can shortcut time and more work can happen. The best helpers, collaborators, or partners are found through strategic networking.

- **Develop vigilance towards uncovering options.** By giving ourselves some quiet time to think and plan, we can be sure that our efforts will be applied to the most advantageous activities.

- **Make choices in our attitudes.** How we deal with our environment (both in control and in letting go) and how we run our businesses will be tested. We can choose how much to let fear inhibit our excitement towards business change and challenge.

- **Stress spirituality** as a strength to draw upon from deep within.

Compared to men, women are more in touch with our bodies, our multiple roles, our self-limiting circumstances, and our culturally-limiting beliefs. This is not to say there isn't much to learn from men. When it comes to wisdom, women have more to learn from other women.

Liane Sebastian

Ms. Sebastian has experience in every facet of graphic arts. As an artist for over 30 years, she has worked as a freelance designer, corporate publishing manager, partner in an award-winning design firm, and now runs a boutique entrepreneurial company. Having served the American Bar Association, Hyatt International Hotels, the Great Books Foundation, the University of Chicago, World Book Encyclopedia, and Smith Bucklin, among many others, she has worked in almost every sector of business. Currently, she specializes in publication and nonprofit design from her Evanston office. ■ Ms. Sebastian has exhibited her drawings, paintings, and prints in national galleries and participates in regional shows. With a passion for publishing, she has authored twelve books, five privately commissioned. Additionally, she speaks at many local and national conferences.

■ *Women Who Win at Work* is designed to showcase experiences in a condensed readable form. ■ She lives and works in Evanston, IL. Please see her design portfolio, art work, and publications at www.prosperiapublishing.com.

Author of: ***Japan in Aspen; The Human Side of Technology; Creative Clienting; The Philosopher of Business: Biography of JimBeré; Ways of Wisdom for Women*** (e-book)***; Idea Initiators, Legacy Ladies, Digital Design Business Practices*** (three editions); and ***Women Who Win at Work.***